· LIFE ·
LESSONS

50 Things I Learned From My Divorce

BETH JOSELOW

AVON BOOKS ◆ NEW YORK

LIFE LESSONS: 50 THINGS I LEARNED FROM MY DIVORCE is an original publication of Avon Books. This work has never before appeared in book form.

AVON BOOKS
A division of
The Hearst Corporation
1350 Avenue of the Americas
New York, New York 10019

Copyright © 1994 by Beth Baruch Joselow
Published by arrangement with the author
Library of Congress Catalog Card Number: 93-50857
ISBN: 0-380-77494-1

Library of Congress Cataloging in Publication Data:

Joselow, Beth.
    Life lessons : 50 things I learned from my divorce / Beth Joselow.
        p.   cm.
1. Divorced women—United States—Life skills guides.   2. Divorced women—United States—Psychology.   3. Separation (Psychology)
I. Title.
HQ834.J47   1994   93-50857
306.89—dc20   CIP

First Avon Books Trade Printing: October 1994

AVON TRADEMARK REG. U.S. PAT. OFF. AND IN OTHER COUNTRIES, MARCA REGISTRADA, HECHO EN U.S.A.

Printed in the U.S.A.

ARC 10   9   8   7   6   5   4   3   2

For Carole, Joni and Maxine, best of the best.
And for Nerie, with thanks and love.

*The stories in this book
are real stories, from real women.
To respect their privacy,
details that might help to identify individuals
have been changed.*

Contents

☙ ☙ ☙

Introduction

❧ ❧ ❧

Oh, life is a glorious cycle of song,
A medley of extemporanea;
And love is a thing that can never go wrong;
And I am Marie of Roumania.
                    —DOROTHY PARKER

In the last twenty-five years or so, the way we view divorce has changed and changed again. Once talked about in whispers as a traumatic and shameful experience of failure, divorce seemed to shed its negative image for a time during the seventies and eighties, when it was applauded as a means of staking a claim for a life of one's own. If a marriage wasn't working well, divorce was thought of as an honest, acceptable, and likely cure. Lose your mate and gain yourself, society seemed to say. The divorce rate soared.

More recently, the losses that inevitably accompany a divorce have been the focus of our attention. After a long period in which we gave each other lots of encouragement to pursue self-fulfillment rather than self-sacrifice, the social tide is turning now toward urging people in troubled relationships to try to work it out, to stay together for the sake of the children.

Divorce is no longer seen as the best cure for a problematical marriage, yet close to half of all marriages in the United States end in divorce even now. We are more aware of the problems a divorce brings with it, but many of us still find that we must end our marriages. Women and men who have made the difficult choice to divorce find themselves on a lonely road, with more questions than answers.

1

It was always a lonely road. In spite of the hundreds of jokes about divorce, the many divorce stories of the rich and famous in the news, and the couples in our neighborhoods that we've watched go through it, most of us know almost nothing about what it's like to end a marriage and begin a new life. Divorce must be a little like a trip to the moon. You can look at the pictures, listen to the stories, examine the specimens brought back to earth. But you can't really know what it's like to go there, until you go there.

After 20 years of marriage, I went through a divorce in 1991. From the day my husband and I separated to about a year after the divorce was final, I felt as if I were walking down a dark road all by myself. Not completely by myself—I had three children who were compelled to make this journey with me. None of us was happy as we started out. We each ran into our own disasters and difficulties along the way, and together we went through a lot of unanticipated changes in our lives.

Each day seemed to bring more fresh surprises—a call from a friend who felt she just had to tell me I was making a mistake, a basement that flooded when the raingutters backed up, a teacher's request for a conference about my child's uncharacteristic poor performance in school. What was going on here? How could I possibly cope?

I got some good advice from lawyers. An accountant and a counselor gave me sound financial and psychological advice. I kept in close touch with the teachers at school. But none of these professionals could explain why I was being led to look so hard at my life every day and find so little in it that was familiar. No one could predict how long this feeling would last.

More than one million American women go through divorce each year. So many of us have been on the same road, and still we so often feel that we are living out this enormous change in our lives all alone. From the difficulty of deciding to divorce (or dealing with someone else's decision), to the trauma and wrangling of the divorce process itself, to the long journey of recovery, we feel odd, isolated, and more than a little lost.

By accident, a few weeks after my husband and I separated, I hit on the best possible thing I could have done for myself. I invited four single women I knew to come to dinner. Two of them were in the middle of getting divorced, one had been divorced for many years, and the fourth had never married. I thought I was seeking them out as single friends, for my newly single life, but their place in my life turned out to be much more crucial than that.

We had a wonderful time at dinner that night, laughing and talking about how we felt about being on our own and what we wanted to accomplish for ourselves. While everyone knew me, most of the others had not met before. By the end of the night we were already in such close touch that everyone asked if they could return again soon. We began to meet regularly once a month.

As the months went by and I lived out the chapters of my own divorce, that group of women friends became my fortress, my cheering section, my mentors, my allies, and the very best group of advice-givers I could ever have imagined. We all functioned that way for each other, and we still do to this day. We have helped each other recover from failed romance, from lost jobs, from lack of self-confidence. We have celebrated weddings, new jobs, and moves to new cities. Together we discovered that we had the power to turn many of the things we cried about together into things we could laugh about together.

When I think about my divorce, I think I couldn't have done it without my many women friends and acquaintances. Someone said something smart about how to choose a lawyer, and I remembered it. Someone else told me that the intense fear of losing everything that kept me awake at night was a phase in the grieving process of divorce, assuring me that I would get through it, just as she had. Another friend warned me about some of the surprising fears her children had had and discussed her problems in facing them. How helpful this was in dealing with my own children's feelings! Someone told me a funny story about her divorce that showed me I could manage this difficult transition without losing my sense of humor. The words of all of these wise women were endlessly sustaining to me. I felt rich with friends.

Anyone going through a breakup needs sympathetic company. Not all women have access to such good friends, especially not during the overheated, painful times of divorce. I hope this book can serve as a kind of support group put between covers. It is written to encourage you as a woman involved in the divorce process to move toward taking charge of your life. It's written to answer some particular questions, to share some individual divorce stories, and to remind you that others have been there before you and that everything will be all right. "Divorce teaches you a lot!" as my friend Constance says. Some of the best of that knowledge follows here.

The advice here comes from the experience of women who were divorced in their twenties, after only a few years of marriage, and women who were divorced in their fifties after raising a family; women who worked out good relationships with their former husbands, and women who didn't; women who remarried, and women who have stayed single; women who were self-supporting, and women who couldn't be.

No one marries with the expectation of divorce. No one can enjoy taking her family apart, altering all of her relationships, facing the future alone. Divorce is an intensely painful experience. Yet it is also an opportunity to grow, to give up a life that has not been working well for a new life that has a better chance to work because it is built from greater self-knowledge and the wisdom that comes only with experience. Every woman in this book has had her share of bad days, and although the stories shared here are stories of successful resolutions to problems, each of us has had problems we were not able to solve quite so well.

Please look at the stories of how we were able to work things out for ourselves and take what you can use from them to build a model for your own future. Every woman in this book has gained self-knowledge, new life skills and self-confidence from making it through the tough passage of divorce. Think of us all as being there to show you that you can make it too. You can. You will.

1.

Be certain you want to divorce.

❧ ❧ ❧

You don't get to decide how you're going to die. Or when.
You can only decide how you're going to live. Now.
                                                    —JOAN BAEZ

Deciding whether to initiate a divorce is one of the toughest
decisions you will ever have to make. Assuming that you are the
one, or one of the two, who wants this change, why do you want
it? Is there another solution to the problems in your marriage that
you would prefer? Do you feel you have exhausted your alternatives? Although you can talk out your situation with friends, family, or a professional counselor, you are finally out there all alone
with this decision. In a way, it is like the decision to marry: You
must make a thorough assessment of your life and decide whether
this is the best course for you. But this time, you don't have the
giddiness of romance to propel you past the uncertainties and am-
biguities that are inevitably a part of such a big decision.

Speaking of romance, don't allow yourself to go too far with the
fantasy of starting a new and more perfect life with a new partner.
Initiating a divorce with the idea that you will soon be rescued by
the "right" mate just isn't realistic. Try imagining life on your own,
in the real world, where you may never find the perfect partner.

What if you have been on the fence for months or even years
about wanting to leave your marriage? How long is long enough
to give it a chance? Giving it a chance may not really have to do
with time, but with looking at your marriage and asking yourself

5

what would have to change in order for you to be content. Then ask yourself whether those changes are possible.

You may be able to help determine how certain you are about wanting to divorce by asking yourself a few key questions.

- ☞ Would you rather be alone than with your mate?
- ☞ Are you willing to face major changes in your lifestyle rather than stay married?
- ☞ Are you prepared to stand firm with your decision in spite of what your mate or others might say about it?

Of course, your answer to each of these questions should be yes, if you are going to proceed with divorce.

Mary, divorced with a three-year-old son after four years of marriage, says, "Don't get a divorce until you can walk away with a bounce in your step. The last few months before I finally left my husband, I went through agony every day—in the morning I'd call the lawyer and say I was ready to file and then by afternoon I'd call him back and cancel. I'd talk to one friend and become wholly convinced that I should stay with my husband and then five minutes later I could talk to another friend and be equally swayed in the opposite direction. Don't make a decision too fast. Just let time pass until you can make a decision easily; the final act should not tear. You should wait until you feel you are walking toward something, not walking away from something."

2.

Learn to accept the inevitable.

❧ ❧ ❧

Since the house is on fire, let us warm ourselves.
—ITALIAN PROVERB

No matter whose decision it is to divorce, your old life is gone for good. The sooner you can accept that, the better. If the decision to divorce was not originally yours, you are faced with the difficulty of accepting an unwanted change.

Some people adapt to change better than others. Some of us like change; some of us dread it. Try to focus on the positive aspects of your new situation. Can you take some pleasure in not having to put up with someone else's bad mood, with cooking what *you* want when you want it, with having more room in the closet? These may seem like little things, but they may help remind you that the cup is half full.

Oddly enough, getting through change successfully may involve *not* thinking as much as thinking. To get through a difficult period, it sometimes helps to turn yourself off for a while if the only thoughts that come to mind are of the *Why me? Why now? How can I possibly cope with this?* variety. Use your strength to push those thoughts away for the time being, at least until you have begun a track record of coping. Take one step at a time, even if that step is just walking to the mailbox and greeting the neighbors. Look at what you have to do only a day, or even an hour at a time, to keep yourself from feeling overwhelmed. Now is not the time to look too far ahead. Too much is in flux. Once you have demonstrated to yourself that you can manage, pull out that evidence and look at it whenever your confidence falters. You coped with your first Saturday night alone? Brava! You went to the PTA meeting by yourself? Good going!

Keep yourself in motion. Don't sit home night after night because it's easier not to face the world. You may just be digging a hole for yourself. Encourage yourself to make plans, to get out and do things. Choose the things that you have always liked to do by yourself or with a friend, or choose new, appealing experiences. You don't have to go to a singles group if you don't want to. What do *you* like to do? Go to the beach for a day. Attend a lecture on the stock market. Take a friend out to shoot some pool. Try something new. Keep yourself healthy.

- Get yourself going on Chapter Two, instead of trying to re-read Chapter One.
- Savor each of your new accomplishments.
- Take it one day at a time.

"I took a long, long time to believe that Mike was really going to go through with this," says Eileen, married twenty-two years with three children. "Months after he had moved out, I still believed he would come back. I kept trying to woo him by inviting him to dinner, by getting a new haircut, new clothes. All I could think about was Mike, even though he gave me no encouragement. My life felt frozen in place. After a few months, Mike refused to come to the house to pick up our youngest son because he said he couldn't deal with the way I'd try to cling to him. He just wasn't connected to us in the same way anymore. I had to let go and accept the fact that my life would never be the same again. I still have trouble accepting that, but I've stopped trying to get my old life back. I'm moving forward."

3.

Expect to be confused.

🐿 🐿 🐿

If you can keep your head when all about you are losing theirs,
it's just possible you haven't grasped the situation.
—JEAN KERR

Maybe you thought you knew what getting divorced was going
to be like. By now, you probably realize how much you didn't
know after all.

You are dealing with many different brand-new life experiences
at once. No doubt you have a lot of questions: How do you tell
other people that you are getting divorced? What should you expect from friends and family members? Should you try mediation
or go straight to a lawyer? When is it time to see one? What can
or can't they do for you? How much is your life going to have to
change? How do the divorce laws in your area work for women?
Is it normal to feel the way you feel about your former mate, about
yourself, about the future?

It's hard to keep your feet under you throughout the divorce
process. It's hard to know all the time whether what you are doing
is right, usual, sensible, similar to what other people have done.
There is no map for divorce, and everyone's journey is a little different from all the others.

It will take some time for you to gain clarity. Most of what you
end up knowing about divorce must be learned through your own
experience. Reading books about the divorce process and talking
to other people will help answer some of your questions, but not

all of them. Other people can give you the benefit of their own experiences, but in some cases you won't take in what they say until you see for yourself, and in other cases their views and attitudes will not match yours.

That feeling of being a stranger in a strange land will subside gradually, as your experience grows. In a way, this passage in your life resembles taking on a new and challenging job. You learn more on the job than you do by having other people tell you what it will be like.

It's hard to have faith that the bad feelings will pass. When you feel like a stranger to yourself, it's difficult to believe that you will once more feel like someone you know well and can count on. But you will.

- Some confusion is par for the course for anyone getting divorced.
- Don't be afraid to ask questions of people who have experienced divorce, or of doctors, accountants, lawyers or other professionals who have specific knowledge.
- Much of what you learn now will be useful for the rest of your life.

Penny, 34, says, "Especially in the beginning, I would be at a party or a meeting and someone would mention that some other person there had been through a divorce, and I would want to rush over and grab that person and bend their ear with all my questions. They always looked so normal and serene. I felt like I was missing a lot of key information that they all knew. Sometimes when I did try to talk to someone like that they'd look at me as if what I was asking them was from out of left field. Our experiences were so different. That could be demoralizing. But sometimes I'd get just a sentence or two from someone that would make a point crystal clear to me. And that was very soothing. It was like finding the next clue in a scavenger hunt. I remember once telling a woman at a school meeting that I was trying to keep sharing parenting with my ex-husband by having him over to the house a lot. She said she thought that would be very uncomfortable and difficult. And it was—I hated it. She said she didn't think that could work out very well, that she'd tried that with her ex-husband for a while and it was too hard. She said she felt better when she started doing things in new ways instead of using her married life as a model. That was a big help. It seemed to give me permission to tell my ex-husband we needed to do things differently."

4.

Get the right lawyer.

∾ ∾ ∾

Hire the best lawyer you can find. A divorce lawyer is a specialist. You will be much better off in the hands of someone who is experienced with all aspects of divorce, from mediation to litigation, than you would be with a lawyer whose real interests are elsewhere, or scattered.

Today, many couples turn to divorce mediation to try to avoid the strife that often accompanies a lawyer vs. lawyer divorce. In some jurisdictions, the law requires a couple to work with a mediator, who works from an objective standpoint to try to help them reach a solution by compromise, before the court will hear their case. Mediation seems to work best for couples who do not have a communication problem—a minority among those seeking divorce.

If you see a mediator first, you will be advised to hire an attorney for yourself before you sign anything. Your attorney will look over the agreement you achieve through mediation to assure that its terms are fair to you. Your husband will have an attorney do the same for him. This step should not be skipped under any circumstances. Let your attorney read the fine print!

Ask friends who have been all the way through the lengthy legal process of divorce for recommendations. Gather as much information as you can about who the good mediators and family law attorneys in town are. Check the library files of local magazines. City magazines often run annual features on the "best" professionals in fields such as divorce law.

Interview several mediators or attorneys. You will have to pay for an hour of their time, but this will be a worthwhile investment. If you think you can't afford that, you really can't afford one who will get you less than the best terms in your settlement. Check out how clearly they explain things, how well they listen to you, how pertinent their questions seem to you, as well as their fees and terms. Don't hesitate to ask questions about how much their time will cost, how much time you are likely to need with them, how much they rely on paralegal assistants to do the bulk of the work in a case like yours, what their track record looks like.

Make sure your lawyer inspires your confidence. In the long run, you may not be saving yourself money by hiring someone who is less experienced and less expensive. Expensive, experienced lawyers often accomplish the same goals more quickly and economically than inexperienced attorneys. They may spend less time on research, or they may delegate the routine work of your case to an assistant. The best lawyers don't waste time. Even if you think your case is relatively simple and not contentious, put yourself in the hands of someone you believe can handle whatever comes along.

At the same time, watch out for lawyers who have the reputation of fighting fire with fire. You should be looking for someone who can give you a balanced, informed perspective on your case, not someone to fan the flames. Make sure you can communicate with the attorney you choose, but don't look for someone you can pour your heart out to. That's a role for a therapist or a best friend. Your lawyer should be someone you can trust with the *business* of your life, because divorce is business, and the people who end up with the best, most workable post-divorce arrangements are the people who treat it like business.

      Get the best representation you can afford. Stretch if you have to.

    🙠 Expect to make many decisions based on experienced legal advice, not to turn over all the decision-making to your lawyer.

    🙠 Be honest with your lawyer or mediator. She can't represent your interests well if you aren't honest.

Katherine, divorced with one child after twelve years of marriage, was on good terms with her husband when they first separated. "I deliberately set out to soften the process by working first with a mediator. That worked pretty well at first, but then my husband refused to participate in the mediation process any more. So I looked for a 'nice' lawyer, one I hoped could keep us from going to war with each other. Big mistake! When my husband flipped out and started making trouble for me—asking for all the furniture in the house, claiming both of our cars were his, just for starters—my lawyer didn't want to make waves. She said why sweat the small stuff? She was exactly what I'd hired her to be—soft. Too soft. It cost me a lot of money, and more grief than I needed at that time, to leave her and find someone who was a good litigator, who didn't advise me to just back down on every point for the sake of a good future relationship with my husband. How could we have a good working relationship if one of us felt we'd been badly taken? My new lawyer knew some strategy for holding the line, and that's what I needed. I still don't think our legal agreement is fair, but it's better than it would have been if I'd followed poor advice."

5.

Put off big decisions.

కు కు కు

There are no signposts in the sea.
—Vita Sackville-West

The first several months after separation are so confusing and uncertain that you will be better off if you can delay making important decisions.

As it is, you are probably having to make a lot of decisions in areas that are new to you, as you simultaneously take apart your past living arrangements and begin to make new ones. Even if decision-making is usually a quick and easy process for you, now is a peculiar time when procrastination may be a virtue.

Some of the problems you face now are going to smooth over and be forgotten sooner than you think. Is your self-esteem suffering? Maybe you shouldn't rush out and buy a new car just to show everyone that you are just fine. Soon enough you will be fine, and your face alone will show it. Wait a while and see if you still want that car enough to pay for it.

It may be tempting, also, to try to make a fresh start in other areas of your life as long as you are in the middle of upheaval. Perhaps you'd like to move to a new city, get a new job, put the past behind you. Those may be entirely reasonable decisions to make. But because divorce is usually such a major change, and highly stressful, now is probably not the best time to make a big career change or to move to the other side of the country, if you can avoid it.

Keeping the other major areas of your life stable for the time being will give you a more secure base from which to survey your situation. Then, when you look out over the horizon and a faraway place beckons to you, you may enjoy the security of knowing that your decision has to do with moving *toward* a new goal, rather than simply away from a bad memory.

Even when you think you're thinking clearly during the early stages of divorce, you may not be. You're on new turf now, and you need to get the lay of the land, to be as fully informed about your present and future prospects as you can be if you are to make the wisest decisions for yourself.

Always remember that you don't have to negotiate, or deal or discuss when you are not feeling up to it. Go away and come back later.

Here are some questions that may help you decide whether a decision is well-timed or not:

- Am I moving away from something old or toward something new in deciding to do this now?
- What will be the consequence of delaying this decision?
- Have I considered all the alternatives to making this particular decision at this particular time?

"Things polarize very quickly when you separate," says Danielle, 39. "A person may want change in the marriage, rather than giving up the marriage permanently. Separation rarely improves a relationship. I was in what I thought was a temporary separation that I had asked for. Evidently my spouse was busy making other plans. Within the first three weeks he presented me with papers to finance a new house he was buying. I had expected him to live somewhere temporarily, anticipating that we would come back together in six months. He said he had to own the place where he lived or it wouldn't feel like a home. He said it would be a good investment. I was at a very vulnerable time and I couldn't make decisions sensibly. Because I didn't want to do anything to drive us further apart, I capitulated. The amount of

debt that was created made settlement much harder later on. But I was not in a position to make a sound decision as to whether or not I should sign the papers so that he could do this. In that emotional state it was not possible for me to make a sound decision. I think he knew that and was moving swiftly before I found my feet. If I had put that off even a few months, I would have said, 'No, I'm sorry. I know you want this but the common welfare is at stake here. There are lots of nice apartments. Once we have settled you can buy anything you want.'"

6.

Get support for yourself.

❧ ❧ ❧

It seems to me that trying to live without friends is like milking a bear to get cream for your morning coffee. It is a whole lot of trouble, and then not worth much after you get it.
—ZORA NEALE HURSTON

There is no reason for you to remain isolated with the problems of getting divorced and building a new life. You have lots of company out there.

In most communities, groups such as Parents Without Partners offer a variety of meetings and services especially for the newly single. Churches, synagogues, women's centers, and community centers often host their own groups as well. If you make a couple of phone calls, you should be well on your way toward finding some very valuable company for yourself among people who have been on the road you are on and have experiences to share.

Another route to explore is counseling. When your life undergoes such a major change, you will have to come to terms with many conflicting emotions and face many hard-to-answer questions. A professional therapist or counselor can be an excellent resource for support, to help you develop the most practical and positive perspective for navigating the rough spots and moving into a promising future. You don't have to commit to anything long-term. You don't have to examine your life from Day One, unless you want to. You can seek counseling to work on the specific issues related to separation and divorce. Ask other divorced women if they can refer you to a good counselor for that purpose.

Most of us have friends and family who rally round when we need them, and they can provide a true lifeline. Now, however, you are likely to need some additional understanding, and some special expertise. You don't have to join a formal group to connect with other women who possess those qualities. If you know a couple of divorced or separated women, even if you don't know them very well, you might ask them to meet for a drink or a cup of tea one afternoon or evening. Many divorced and separated women are eager to "network" with women who share their experience, and eager to give each other support.

When you feel like a little boat out on the big, dark sea, it's quite comforting to look over at lots of other boats sailing along beside you.

- ✺ Difficulties are often made easier by having understanding company as you tackle them.
- ✺ Now may be an excellent time to get support from professional counseling.
- ✺ Don't hesitate to let your need for company and advice be known to other women who have been separated or divorced. Most will be eager to share their experience.

"Anne and I met because she put an ad up at the Y that said, 'If you're a single parent and you want to get together, please call,' " says Claudia, 32. "Now we're on a mission to find other single parents. We live in a kind of perfect neighborhood where it seems as if in every other house the dad is a successful executive and the mom is beautiful and stays at home to drive her two children's carpools in her four-wheel-drive vehicle. They couldn't possibly be divorced! They're too successful! I know that lots of them do get divorced, but meanwhile I feel like I'm on a very different track out there. So Anne and I get together with our kids every week. And we have a wonderful time. We completely understand what each of us is going through. We found

two other women in our search and now we have dinner with them once a month. Next week we're all having a bowling and pizza night with our kids. We don't really help each other materially—we're all too busy! But we pass on advice and useful 'coping' information. Spiritually it's a wonder. When I see our nights coming up on the calendar I feel like I'm looking at the light at the end of the tunnel."

7.

Make the most of being alone.

✿ ✿ ✿

*Alone, alone, oh! We have been warned about solitary vices.
Have solitary pleasures ever been adequately praised? Do
many people know that they exist?*

—JESSAMYN WEST

Being alone or on your own with children is one of those "is
the cup half full or half empty?" situations. That is, it's as good or
as bad as your point of view. Luckily, your point of view is ad-
justable.

You can work on not being alone. But you are also going to
have to learn how to be alone. Even when you devote a great deal
of effort to getting an active social life going, there will be times
when no one is available to go to dinner or a movie, or when you
come home at the end of an evening and home seems more quiet
and empty than you can bear.

It's important to get through those times without letting anxiety
or sheer loneliness get the better of you. If you find yourself dreading evenings alone, start a project. Build a ship in a bottle. Make
a soufflé. Study Italian. Set some goals for your projects and reward yourself when you meet them. If you use some of this down
time to get things done that you didn't have time for before, you'll
be giving your ego the benefit of pride in accomplishment.

It's even okay to keep the television on all night if you just want
the sound of other people around you. It's okay to catch up on old
movies, lagging correspondence, and personal beautification plans.

Keep busy. Don't let yourself spend night after night brooding or mourning. Although it's good to think things through, do your thinking on a trip to the market or a long walk in the park. At night, we are all more vulnerable to sadness and depression. Try to choose activities that will help you lighten up on evenings alone.

Be daring. Take a weekend away at a bed and breakfast by yourself. Drive out into the country to scout antiques. Sign up for scuba diving lessons. Why not? The activity will be fun, and again, you'll boost your ego by stepping up to life.

- List the advantages of time alone for yourself and read your list over.
- Plan in advance how to spend weekends alone. Don't let them sneak up on you.
- Choose rewarding activities, not just catching up on chores, for your alone time, so that you will begin to look forward to it.

"My older son was eighteen, starting his first year of college, and my younger son was fifteen and starting his first year of high school when my husband left," says Mina, 49. "He actually moved out when I was out of town on a business trip and didn't tell anybody he was leaving. He'd been involved with someone else, and I'd known about it for a while. At that particular point I had had some vague goal of trying to get him to stay until the boys were both off to college, because it was so close to the end of our child-raising. You know," she laughs, "it was sort of like staying in the military those extra three years to get the retirement. Not that it was a wonderful relationship or anything. But when I came home and saw that he had moved out, I was stunned. And to top it off, my mother died entirely unexpectedly, three weeks later. What a year! I was reeling, and terrified, mostly about money and practical things. But then, after a little while, I would realize, usually when I got into bed at night— I'd get all my pillows around me, and my book, and the remote control for the TV, and I'd think 'Oh boy, this is wonderful. This is the best-kept secret.' I love

living alone. My younger son left for college this year so that leaves me and the cat. And I just love it. It's been five years since my separation. I'm in a nice relationship now, but I love to live alone. I'm amazed because I was really dreading having my younger son leave for school. But I have to admit, I never want to share a bathroom with a man again! If I do live with anyone else again I will be much more respectful of my own enjoyment and need for my own space and control over my own life.''

8.

Avoid dangerous shortcuts
to divorce.

   ϟ   ϟ   ϟ

I am extraordinarily patient, provided I get my own way in the end.

                    —MARGARET THATCHER

A complicated task simply can't be rushed. If you try to rush it, something almost always gets botched. If you are not a patient person, you are probably better off not trying to tailor a suit or teaching your teenager to drive. Let someone else do those things.

Alas, if you're involved in a divorce, you don't have the option of getting someone else to do it for you. You will have to see it through. And you will have to be patient.

Even if it was a short marriage, your marriage was built over a long period of time. Its structure is complex. If you don't want it to just fall down around you (or worse, *on* you), you will have to deconstruct it with care and attention.

If you've reached the point of initiating a divorce, you may wish it could all be over tomorrow. It can't and it won't.

One way or another, you will have to live out all of the stages of divorce. Even if you've decided that you just want to be done with it as soon as possible, the only part of it that you can really hurry is the legal side.

The danger there is that you may agree to terms that, in the long run, are not in your best interest. Your present self may just want

24

to put a painful situation behind you as soon as possible. You may be willing to sacrifice almost anything just to be free. But what about your future self? Are you able now to carefully consider her needs? She's counting on you.

Take your time. What seems so crucial right now may lose its urgency sooner than you think. Don't jeopardize a secure future just to get there more quickly. Look after yourself well.

Even if you go after a quick divorce decree, you should realize that emotional transformations take a long time. How long? As long as they take. There's no way around it: you just have to be patient. You'll get there. We all do.

- ∂ Patience is a virtue you must cultivate.
- ∂ There is no such thing as a quick divorce. Emotional journeys take time.
- ∂ Don't set yourself up for lifelong problems by rushing to put your present pain behind you.

"Take your time," says Elena, 46. "When we first separated, my husband and I put together a temporary one-year agreement. I wanted a temporary agreement because I didn't feel like making decisions for my kids, who at that time were eleven and thirteen, for the rest of their lives, and I didn't really feel like I knew enough or that I was sane enough to make long-term decisions. So my husband and I agreed to make whatever decisions we could make for one year and to negotiate a final divorce agreement after that. I was really glad I did that. I learned not to make any agreement to anything on the spur of the moment—to go home, to think about it. And yet, in spite of how careful I was, I wasn't quite patient enough. I got sick and tired of negotiating so after a while I took what I could get today and I didn't look after tomorrow. So I had no provision for my kids' college education. At the time, it was still several years off and that seemed like a long time. But when we got to that time, I didn't have the same bargaining power with my former husband and it was hard to get him

to share the expense for college. That was a real problem for the first few years of my daughter's education. I made a conscious choice to give up the future for the here and now. I'd probably try to be more balanced now."

9.

Keep the big picture in focus.

ॐ ॐ ॐ

To work in the world lovingly means that we are defining what we will be for, rather than reacting to what we are against.
—CHRISTINA BALDWIN

Even the most calm, cool-headed people find it hard to keep an objective perspective when they feel pelted with problems, challenges, and difficult decisions day after day over a long period of time.

You are dismantling a large part of the structure of your life when you bring a marriage to an end. At the same time, you are laying the foundation for the structure your life will have from now on. You must keep what you intend to build in mind even as you take things apart. That is not an easy assignment.

Everyone involved in a divorce is operating under pressure and stress and is likely to demonstrate some emotional extremes. If your former mate calls you names, your immediate response may be to fire off a nasty letter to him, listing all your complaints about him and then some. Think carefully before you take that step, or do anything else that could widen the rift between you. The two of you still have a lot to work out with each other.

If friends let you down by not understanding exactly what you're going through, think about the history of your friendship with them before you tell them never to darken your doorstep again. Are they people you've felt close to for some time? Can you picture them in your future, after everything has calmed down?

As often as possible, every response that you make to the situation you are in now should be made with the long term in mind. If you decide to move back to your hometown because you really, really need someone to take care of you right now, how long are you prepared to stay? What kind of life would you be able to establish for yourself there? If you were to change your mind after a few weeks or a few months there, would you still have a job and a home to return to?

Don't burn all your bridges while your emotions are aflame. Try to look as far down the road as possible when you are preparing to take action, or when you respond to someone else's action. Taking the long view will help you be calmer and more objective. You will come out ahead for it.

- ❧ Ask yourself where you want to be when this is all over before you make any big decisions.
- ❧ Whenever you feel done in by today, look as far down the road toward tomorrow as you can.
- ❧ When you feel tempted to blow off some steam, think of the long-term effect that would have on your relationships.

Brenda, 44, was divorced when her twin daughters were seven years old. "For a while after we separated, my mother-in-law called me up about once a week to tell me what a terrible thing it was for Marty and me to be getting divorced. She said why didn't I just get some sexy new nightgowns and try to work things out. She was unbelievably insulting, and nosy and infuriating. Our divorce was not easy in a lot of ways and I was feeling very put upon, working hard, dealing with the girls' feelings. One night I just exploded at her and told her never to call me again. And for about a week or two I was very happy not to have to listen to her. But she is a really good grandmother. She loves my girls, and they enjoy her company. And we all live just a couple of miles apart. Did I really want the girls to have to give her up because she made me mad? So I wrote her a letter, and I told her I was sorry I had exploded at her. But I also gave her certain ground rules for how we could relate to each other. I told her I didn't want to hear any more of her questions or her criticism. Then she called me and we were all in touch again. I had to remind her quite a few times that she was not to bring up certain subjects with me, but it has worked out well. I really can't imagine what it would have been like to try to keep her away from the girls. That would have been terribly unfair to everyone. It's lucky for all of us that she loves them so much, and now I can even enjoy their pleasure in her, even if she and I will never be best friends. She's a wonderful grandmother."

10.

Get past the need for vengeance.

❧ ❧ ❧

Something of vengeance I had tasted for the first time; as aromatic as wine it seemed, on swallowing, warm and racy; its afterflavor, metallic and corroding, gave me a sensation as if I had been poisoned.

—CHARLOTTE BRONTË

It's hard to avoid fantasies of revenge on someone who has given you pain and distress. So don't avoid them. Fantasize away. It's probably good for your mental health.

Real revenge is another matter. There is absolutely no lasting benefit to engaging in acts of vengeance on your former mate or anyone else related to the end of your marriage. For one thing, you need your self-respect. Every ounce of pride you can summon in yourself will be put to good use to sustain and strengthen you during the divorce process. Acting vengefully, while it may provide momentary feelings of triumph, rarely results in feeling good about yourself. You don't have to turn the other cheek. You can just walk away clean.

If you and your former mate have children, you must do what you can to keep their relationship with their father civilized and healthy. Even if it has been necessary for you to keep your contact with him to a minimum, make sure that, at least on your part, all of your contact is polite. You can be as cold as ice if he's making trouble for you, but don't fall into the trap of trying to get back at him for what he does. You will risk having your battles escalate beyond your control. And that will be damaging for everyone.

Concentrate on building rather than demolishing. Focus on creating a good life for yourself. Smile with the satisfaction of knowing that living well really is the best revenge. After a while, you won't even need those vengeful fantasies.

- Rise above the desire to even the score.
- You can defeat those petty acts of meanness by ignoring them.
- Don't look at what he's done to you. Look at what you can do for you.

Ellen and Nick had been married for seven years when they agreed that their marriage wasn't working and decided to separate. "Nothing went smoothly," says Ellen, 34. "Nick insisted on staying in the house, so my daughter and her babysitter and I all moved in with my parents. Even that didn't satisfy Nick, though. Within a week, he barged into my folks' house, got into a huge argument with me and ended up knocking me to the floor. That was all I needed. I filed charges against him for assault that afternoon. After that, it seemed as if I spent most of my time fending off problems with Nick. He stopped paying his share of the bills, he repeatedly called me up to yell at me, and he took me back to court twice—to reduce child support, to get visitation changed—just to make life difficult. But I've learned a valuable lesson from all this: you can't let it overwhelm your life. You have to let it go. Sure you're angry and resentful, but you just have to let it go. There are other things in life. You have to go on and find the things that are good for you and go after those things. My ex-husband is always going to be a nutcase, he's always going to hassle me. He's told me that. He continues this process through lawyers and through the courts. I can't change him. I can only change my attitude. And I like myself enough that I want to do whatever I must to live a light-filled life, not a life dominated by anger and resentment. So I work at it. My business is doing well and I love my work. My daughter is the light of my life. These are the things I want to think about, so that's where I put my effort."

11.

Learn to distinguish guilt from responsibility, and get rid of guilt.

ॡ ॡ ॡ

Mistakes are part of the dues one pays for a full life.
—SOPHIA LOREN

There isn't much you can do with guilt, other than to forgive it and move on. Everyone makes mistakes. The best thing to do with your mistakes is to figure out what they were about so that you can at least try not to repeat them.

In a way, guilt makes things too easy for you. It allows you to settle for feeling bad instead of doing the work of analyzing your mistakes. Instead of feeling guilty about your contribution to the end of your marriage, try sitting yourself down with pencil and paper to sort out what your actual responsibilities were, and what your former husband's responsibilities were. No one ends a marriage all by himself or herself.

Ask yourself exactly where you messed up in your marriage. Look for concrete and specific points, rather than vague generalizations. It's more useful to say, for example, "I didn't express my feelings of affection as openly or as often as he wanted me to," than it is to say, "I'm not nice enough." You can learn something from admitting, "I was afraid of talking about things that bothered me so I went around in a pout too much of the time," but you can't learn much from telling yourself, "I'm a moody, difficult person."

Look at things that you did or didn't do. Don't assassinate your own character. Good people make mistakes too!

If you try to be as honest as you can in making your list, it may actually turn out to consist of just a couple of things, a couple of behavior patterns or ways of thinking or expressing yourself that you can now try to alter.

Now you can go over those things in your friendships, or in new intimate relationships and bring with you what you have learned from experience.

- Figure out what went wrong rather than try to hide everything under one big blanket of guilt.
- Sort out what you might have done differently from what was beyond your control.
- Give yourself credit for being able to learn from experience.

"I was the one to end my marriage and the final way, the final gesture was to have an affair," says Patricia, 51. "Everything got focused on that in me and in my ex-husband so that we didn't focus on an eleven-year marriage. It was as if that event alone had ended our marriage. So I still had work to do to find out where I was responsible, to segregate out that one event and not to look at it as if everything led to that one event. I had to take responsibility for that event, to realize I had done something irrevocable when I started that affair. But I also had to separate that from the responsibility we both shared for problems in the marriage. Responsibility is a really good thing. Responsibility smells different from guilt. You have to learn the difference. There were things I needed to be responsible for that I did and didn't do in that relationship. Thinking those things through has been enormously helpful to me in my present marriage. You will bring the same personality into new relationships. You can learn from your experience what your usual pitfalls are and learn not to fall into them again. You can learn not to repeat your patterns. You might say 'I was perfect and he was a jerk,' or even vice versa, but that's not usually the case."

12.

Act the way you want to feel.

ॐ ॐ ॐ

It is hard to fight an enemy who has outposts in your head.
—SALLY KEMPTON

As you map out the new territory of your life, you will be faced with lots of uncertainties and lots of things you can't control. One very valuable resource that you should be able to direct, however, is your attitude. It takes practice, but you can learn to have faith in yourself in a way that will strongly boost your ability to meet the challenges of change.

It's simple but true that if you put on a happy face, you will feel happier. If you give yourself a pep talk about how capable you are, you will feel more capable. You've probably noticed that when you wear clothes you like, you feel more powerful in the world. The same goes for putting on a self that you like. When you like yourself, you feel more energetic, and you project an energy that draws others to you.

It's hard to like yourself all the time when you're in the middle of a divorce. It's hard to keep a positive outlook when you feel besieged by expected and unexpected problems. At times, you're going to have to pump yourself up.

Just when you feel, "I can't do this," is the time to stand in front of the mirror and tell yourself that you *can* do it. Getting through a tough day successfully means following the model of the successful job interview: walk in looking cool and confident, and eager to succeed.

35

Instead of letting yourself put on that navy blue suit again, or those old comfortable jeans and a sweater, choose something else from your closet, something colorful that you always feel good in. Get a haircut. Change your glasses, or get yourself some fabulously flattering sunglasses. This is not to suggest that you have yourself "made over" or undergo some kind of radical change in your style. Don't try to be someone other than yourself, but give yourself the chance to be your *best* self, the self you like most. Then you will be better equipped for whatever you have to face today. And if you're better equipped, you are more likely to succeed, and the next day will be easier than today.

- ✺ The way you act can dramatically alter the way you feel about yourself, for the better.

- ✺ Acting upbeat and positive will help you gain support from other people.

- ✺ The success you achieve by acting the way you want to feel is sure to build on itself, until you no longer have to *act* as if you feel successful.

Susan is thirty-seven and has two children, seven and five years old. She says, "When Rob and I split up, I had been home with the girls for a few years. The only work I had done was as an aide at the pre-school they both attended. All of a sudden I had to figure out how to make a full-time wage. I had been a legal secretary in the old days before we had kids, but offices hadn't run on computers and FAX machines then. So if I was going to trade on my old skills, I knew I had to sell myself to a firm that would be willing to give me some on-the-job training. In some ways, the timing was awful. I'd never felt like such a failure in my life, and I had more to cope with than ever— taking care of the house on my own, the car, dealing with lawyers for myself for the first time in my life. When I thought about going into a law firm again after so many years, I didn't know if I could dare compete with all those well-trained kids. But I didn't have much of a choice. I had to get out there and sell myself. I called people I had

*worked for in the past and was able to get some leads on job possibil-
ities. On the mornings when I had interviews set up I'd wake up in a
complete panic. Then I'd put on something I felt especially good in,
tell myself that I was a professional, with lots of experience—which
was true, even if I was a little out of the mainstream then. I'd try to
convince myself at least temporarily that I was the best thing since
sliced bread. Then I'd go out to meet a bunch of strangers. I'd show
them my work history and tell them why I could do a better job for
them than anyone else could. The more I talked, the more I believed it.
And one of them finally believed it, too, and gave me a job. Once I got
in the door, things started to click again; the atmosphere felt familiar.
I got up to speed pretty quickly with word processing and I discovered
that I like it. And I like my job. So I don't have to pretend to like
myself anymore—I really do."*

13.

Face problems squarely and only when necessary.

≈ ≈ ≈

'Tain't worthwhile to wear a day all out before it comes.
—SARAH ORNE JEWETT

There will be days when you feel as if you're faced with approximately three million pressing problems. How are you ever going to solve them all? One at a time, and only as needed.

If that sounds like a prescription, it is. You can't let yourself think about all your problems at once. You will only put yourself in a panic. You can't solve problems when you're panicking.

Begin by using the divide-and-conquer method. Separate your concerns into two groups: short term and longer term.

Under the first heading, you may be looking at issues such as how to tell friends and family about the divorce, who you can ask to show you how to change the filters on the furnace without your having to feel helpless, or how to pay for the new fuel pump your car suddenly demands.

On the long-term list may be such issues as how to get your new social life started, how you can earn enough money to maintain a comfortable lifestyle, whether you should relocate to a different city or a new neighborhood.

If today's the day when your fuel pump broke, start by solving that problem. That's enough for today. Don't let your mind dash from who's going to fix it, to how you're going to pay for it, to how you really ought to look for a better-paying job, to how you don't know how to meet new people, to whether you should pull up stakes and head west. Just fix the fuel pump. Then let yourself feel good about having solved that problem. And when you let yourself really see that you *can* problem-solve, when you are feeling good about yourself as a capable, independent woman, *then* you can let yourself think about those long-range issues. Little by little, the solutions will make themselves known to you, especially if you can keep your priorities clear and try to stay relaxed.

- Don't try to solve all your problems at once.
- Focus on what needs doing right away. Let long-range concerns go until you feel confident about taking them on.
- Bask in the good feeling of having solved a problem before you rush on to the next one. You'll boost your confidence tremendously.

"I used to go into a tailspin about once a week, just overwhelm myself with thoughts of all I had to deal with," says Marcella, 38. "My two sons were still in elementary school and I felt very strongly that I didn't want to uproot them. I had been home with them and didn't feel I had any good job skills, and Tim and I were going to have to sell the house to make our property division. I didn't know what to worry about first. And then, of course, there were all the little daily problems that came up. I'd lie awake at night counting my problems like sheep! I was a wreck just from lack of sleep. So I began to get out of bed and write down everything I needed to take care of. Then I would put the list in order, according to which ones I needed to take care of that week. I put the less urgent things at the bottom of the list, to wait for me to get to them later. Just knowing that I had them all organized like that helped me put them aside and get to sleep. When I was in a calm frame of mind, I was able to be pretty inventive about solving some of our biggest problems. I worked out an arrangement with Tim so we could stay in the house until the boys finished elementary school. And as part of that deal, I got him to give us more

support while I went back to school and became an occupational ther-apist. So then when we did have to sell the house and move, I repaid Tim, and by then I felt much more ready and competent to manage more by myself."

14.

Take care of your health.

ৰ৶   ৰ৶   ৰ৶

I believe that the physical is the geography of the being.
—LOUISE NEVELSON

Stress takes its toll on our bodies, and divorce is one of the most stressful life passages you may ever go through. Now is the time to be alert to messages from your body, and to make some moves to keep stress from causing further distress.

Your past experience with coping with short-term crises or anxieties may have given you some ideas for how you can most effectively deal with stress. Taking time out for a long soak in the tub or going for a long walk may be very therapeutic. Getting away from it all for a weekend in the country may be ideal.

If your experience parallels that of most women, the process of getting divorced will be two or more years long. And that's just the "on the record" time. You will do well to plan a long-term stress-relief program for yourself.

The benefits of taking an hour at least three times a week to put your heart and muscles through some kind of aerobic activity will be enormous, and especially valuable to you now. Not only will you reduce your risk for illness, but you will achieve some instant relief from anxiety and depression. And you're sure to look better, too, a guaranteed lift to the spirit!

Exercise also gives you a reason to get away from your daily tasks and focus on yourself for an hour or two. Make it a requirement of your work week. Remember, it's important to your health:

Don't think of it as "time off" but time *on* in the job of taking care of yourself. You can slow down your thinking and allow for some productive meditation while you're swimming laps or bicycling. You can have some laughs and find some good company by taking an aerobics class. Choose an activity that you can really enjoy, not one that will feel like a chore.

Nothing bad can come of adding regular exercise to your schedule. It can only help you feel better, mentally *and* physically.

- Check with your doctor about what kind and how much exercise would be most beneficial to you.
- Think of exercise as a requirement, not a luxury, in your weekly schedule.
- Choose activities that feel more like fun than work to you. It's okay to have fun during a crisis. In fact, it's good for you.

"I didn't have any health problems but I certainly was stressed out in the first few months," says Margo, 56. "A friend said I should get some exercise, that it was important for mental health. So I started hiking and that's very much part of my life now. I'd hiked as a teenager and never really liked it. But I do a lot of hiking now. I have two children who also are hikers so we go hiking together. We just came back from a trip to New Zealand hiking. The kids said they were going and they asked me to join them. We've hiked in Yosemite, too. I just went hiking all day Sunday. It's made a tremendous difference. I love to do it. I go with a group always. I never go by myself, but I like to put myself in the middle with people ahead of me and behind me so I feel comfortable for safety and yet I feel I'm by myself. At the end of a hiking day the world looks absolutely wonderful and I feel like I can accomplish anything. And my body has changed shape. I don't have to worry about what I eat as much. I hike at least once a week and take long walks every chance I get. I walk with a friend, or by myself. Yesterday in the pouring rain I walked a mile and a half to the subway. I guess I was feeling stressed because in spite of the rain I felt such a strong urge to walk. It really helped."

15.

Keep your sense of humor.

✑ ✑ ✑

Total absence of humor renders life impossible.
—COLETTE

A sense of humor is really a sense of perspective. As long as you can laugh at what hurts, at least some of the time, you know that you are keeping your balance.

Divorce breeds chaos. Because the whole process is so unsettling, it is likely to bring you at least a few nights when you forget to put the windows up in the car and it rains on the upholstery all night, or you put the dog out and bring the garbage in. For a while you may have a string of days when your hair looks like it was styled on Mars and you can't find the belt to your best suit, and the notes for the speech you have to make this afternoon are sitting on the kitchen counter dotted with peanut butter.

Be patient with yourself. Step back from your situation for a minute and take a look at it. If it weren't happening to you, it would be hilarious. Transitions are seldom neat and tidy. Some mistakes can teach us lessons. Others can only be laughed at.

Your sense of humor can be good company for you. It's no joke that laughter is the best medicine.

What's more, the spirit and attitude you project throughout the time of divorce will show your friends and acquaintances that you *are* good company—or not. You need their support and companionship now, no doubt. You're likely to get more of it if you show them that you can be fun to be with.

This is not to say that you need to put on a false front for everyone. Sometimes you may feel too down to be good company for anyone. Sometimes you may need to talk out your troubles with a close friend. But you do need to be conscious of the overall impression you give to other people. If they see that you can still laugh at yourself, they will feel more confident of enjoying your company, and they will be available to you more often.

But most of all, the best of *you* will be available to you and *you* will enjoy your own company more yourself.

- Allow yourself to see what's laughable around you. Then allow yourself a good laugh.
- Remember: Laughter heals.
- Call up your good friends when you have something funny to relate, not just when you need a shoulder to cry on.

"This sounds unbelievable, but it really happened," Holly says. She had been separated for about six months from her husband of eleven years when she and her two sons came home after a weekend away. "I'd taken the kids away for the weekend because I was feeling completely overwhelmed by all the stuff that was going wrong. The kids' dad and I could barely speak to each other. They were starting to cut the workforce at my office. And I had a weird rash I was afraid might be the start of something serious. So I just went off to forget about it all. When we got home, I put my key in the door and turned the lock, but then I still couldn't get the door open. I pushed and pushed, and I could feel some big heavy thing in the way of the door. I couldn't imagine what it was. Finally, I put my shoulder into the door and gave it one big shove. It opened just enough for me to squeeze through, and to trip over the rubble that filled the living room. Somehow, for no known reason, the ceiling had caved in while we were away! Can you believe it? I just sat down and cried. Then I called my friend Nancy and said, 'Guess what? The sky really is falling!' She laughed so hard when I told her what had happened that I couldn't help laughing myself. It was just so unbelievable, and fitting. It was

a pain in the neck to get everything cleaned up and repaired. But it sure makes a good story! I really do believe in fate, and I think it was a great cosmic joke for that to happen with what was going on at the time."

16.

Be prepared: The law is not always fair and it doesn't cover everything.

☙ ☙ ☙

There's a world of difference between truth and facts. Facts can obscure the truth.

—MAYA ANGELOU

Working out the terms for settlement in divorce is usually difficult, complicated, and frustrating. It's important to attend to the process carefully. The legal agreements you reach are likely to have some effect on the rest of your life.

You cannot put yourself in the hands of the law, or even in the hands of a good lawyer, and expect to get an agreement that will seem completely fair to you. For one thing, you have knowledge about your individual situation that is different and more thorough than the knowledge your lawyer or the court will ever have. Law has a relatively narrow view of things, and is written so that emotional and personal views will not have much effect on legal decisions. In court, most decisions about property are based on numbers, not on what anyone thinks is "fair."

The laws governing separation and divorce and division of assets differ from jurisdiction to jurisdiction. When you are ready to seriously consider settlement, take the time to thoroughly educate yourself about the laws in your state. In some states, for example, mothers of children under age eighteen have the right to remain in the family home until the eighteenth birthday of their youngest child. In other states, sale of the family home may be enforced by laws calling for equal division of assets at the time of divorce, with no delay allowed. This does not mean that you cannot get a delay in those jurisdictions, however. That is why you have a lawyer— to use the law to attempt to get what you think you need for a livable future.

It's almost always best to work out the terms of your settlement with your former mate, rather than to let the court decide on those issues for you. Each of you knows things about your particular circumstances that may call for more creative solutions and compromises than any court could ever come up with for you. No judge could be expected to understand your situation as thoroughly as the two of you do, nor will the law allow a judge to make the kind of concessions you can make to each other when you agree on a common good.

Your lawyer will probably urge you to try to negotiate as much of your settlement outside of court as possible. Take that advice seriously. In most cases, a negotiated settlement meets the needs of both parties far better than does a court battle. Little satisfaction or vengeance can be gained by taking each other to court. That should be a last resort.

Negotiation doesn't mean capitulation. Remember:

- You don't have to negotiate when you don't feel up to it. Wait until you feel clear-headed and able to stand up for yourself.
- Don't expect the law to see things your way.
- Dealing with the law calls for putting emotion aside as much as possible and using your business head to settle on agreeable terms.

Renee, 49, divorced eleven years ago when her three children were all under the age of twelve. She tried to work out as many details as possible with her former husband before bringing the law to bear on their settlement. "We each had a lawyer in the end," she says, "but we negotiated most of the agreement ourselves and we didn't spend much money and we didn't go to court. Looking back on it, I'm surprised that we were able to do that, because our communication at the time was not that great. We were sort of pushed into it because we didn't have much money and couldn't afford to just hand the thing over to lawyers from the beginning and let them go at it. We were lucky, in a way, because we ended up agreeing on certain things that were very much to the kids' advantage and which the law in our area would not have dealt with the way we did. And it also gave us a basis for continuing to collaborate on things that concerned the kids, which we've had to do often, even though neither of us wishes to have any kind of lively friendship with each other. I was furious with him when we were getting divorced, but I'm glad I didn't just try to get the law after him. I don't think it would have done anybody any good. This is much better."

17.

Go after what you want in your settlement, and get it in writing to avoid future arguments.

ॐ ॐ ॐ

No one can build his security on the nobleness of another person.

—Willa Cather

One point worth returning to is that the negotiated aspects of divorce are the business aspects, and they should be treated as business. Much that you have to sort through is emotional and personal. Dividing property and making arrangements to support children, however, involve the use of good business sense.

You can accommodate your former mate emotionally as much as you like, but not in this area. When you consider the terms of settlement, you must view your circumstances as objectively as possible and think about what you really need to give yourself and your children a good basis for the future.

It is a common characteristic of women to be peacemakers, compromisers, fixers. These are admirable and useful qualities when they function appropriately. In figuring out your settlement, however, you must begin by making an honest appraisal of your needs, *without* first thinking of the needs of your former mate. No doubt, you will have to compromise before an agreement is reached. Don't begin by trying to second-guess the points of compromise and offering to give up more than you want or need to give up. Begin by taking a strong stand for what you need and believe is your fair share in your settlement.

Most of us have been faced with particular sticking points as we tried to reach an agreement with our former mates. Trying to get past these points by taking them out of the negotiation or leaving them for later is probably not a good idea. Leaving the issue of who pays college costs for later, even if your children are just toddlers, is a mistake. Now is the time when your relationship to each other is live and clear to all of you. Now is the time when the questions of this continuing relationship should be resolved, and the resolution made part of your written agreement, particularly where finances are concerned.

By seeing things through now you will cut down on years of uncertainty in the future, cut down on the possibility of someone losing interest in the issue and refusing to address it later (when it is sometimes too late and often too expensive to bring the law into it), cut down on the agenda of things you may continue to argue about.

It is not distrustful or disrespectful to ask for everything in writing. It is smart—and respectful of the future.

- ∾ Don't be afraid to ask for what you want in your settlement.
- ∾ Get it in writing *now*.
- ∾ Respect the terms of your written agreement, just as you want them to be respected in turn.

"My child-support check is deposited automatically from his account into mine on the day it is due," says Jaye, mother of two. "He works for a company that makes that possible. Karl is a person who spends to his last nickel. He has a great stereo, but if he sees one that is one notch better, out comes his credit card. He never has money. When the kids ask him for anything, he never has money. He's always broke even though he makes a lot of money. No matter how much he made, it would be the same. I knew that I would be in deep trouble if

he had to present me with a check at the first of the month because he'd say to me, 'I don't have it right now. Let me give it to you in two weeks, let me give it to you in a month.' But I couldn't say that to him because of course it would have immediately rubbed him the wrong way. So what I said was, 'Look, for me it's humiliating to ask you for money. For my sense of self-esteem, I need not to have that transaction.' And he agreed and signed off on the direct-deposit method. That means that the money is always there, and we don't fight about it. He wants to take care of his kids, and this makes that easier."

18.

Don't try to take care of your former mate, or try to have him take care of you.

❧ ❧ ❧

If my hands are fully occupied in holding on to something, I can neither give nor receive.

—DOROTHEE SÖLLE

Most women are practiced caretakers, having been socialized if not born to attend to the needs of others. And in most marriages, wives have been sensitive to the needs of their husbands and have done their part to meet them. Husbands, too, have developed caretaking instincts for their wives.

When a marriage is ending, many accustomed roles have to be left behind by both partners. The man who continues to come to his former home to mow the lawn is delaying final acceptance of the fact that it is no longer his home. The woman who continues to run errands for her estranged husband because it seems simple enough is delaying her own acceptance of the idea that she will no longer be his wife.

Most people are more than happy to accept being cared for, and caretaking can be generous and virtuous. But at times, both the caretaker and the cared for may be impeding their own growth and progress by continuing to cooperate in roles that are no longer appropriate or helpful to either of them.

If your goal is to reach an amicable conclusion to your marriage, you will not make any progress toward that end by pretending that nothing has changed.

You can still offer kindness and consideration without trying to take care of each other. It is kind and considerate to keep your former mate up to date on important moments you have witnessed with your children. But cooking dinners for him to put in his freezer might be a counterproductive kind of caretaking, because it delays the growth of independence for each of you.

If both of you wish to have a good relationship in the future, you will be able to work that out without either of you having to continue to take care of the other. If you are able to remain reasonably civil with each other throughout the divorce process, you will retain the basis for a decent post-divorce friendship. But at some point, if each of you is really to move on in your life, you must give up relying on each other for the kind of caretaking that is more often part of marriage.

You must now look to others, not to each other, for emotional support if you are truly to make the break. And you must learn to cook, install washers in the faucets, and deal with recalcitrant repair people on your own or with the help of a good friend. Once you have achieved independence, and some perspective on your marriage and its conclusion, you will be in a better position to forge a new, strong relationship with your former mate.

- Respect your former mate by believing that he can make it without your caretaking.
- Respect yourself as well, by showing that you too can live independently.
- Clear the ground for a new, healthy relationship with your former mate by not trying to hang on to the habits and routines of your old relationship.

"When we were married," says Jackie, 41, "I was always the one in charge of finances. I made the monthly budget and put aside whatever

*savings we could each month. I handled the tax returns, health insur-
ance claims, all that. We are both teachers, so it was relatively clear-
cut. When we separated, I moved out to my own apartment for a while.
Since Jim had the house and the two children at that time, I thought
it was only fair for me to give him some money each month for the
mortgage and other household expenses. We had a pretty quiet separation, no big quarrels. But as summer approached, I realized that I
was leaving myself with no savings to get through summer, when I
wouldn't be getting a paycheck until September. Jim worked for another district, and he continued his pay through the summer. So I just
told him I had to look after my own needs now, and I stopped giving
him money. I realized I had been doing that just to make myself feel
better about moving out anyway, as if I was saying 'I'm moving out
but don't worry, I won't let you down.' Even after that, I kept on
doing both our taxes, right up to the time when our divorce became
final and we weren't filing jointly anymore. It wasn't such a big problem for us to finally make these changes, but until we did, we—or I,
at least— were essentially putting off the finality of things. We have
a relationship still. Now it's a different kind of relationship. Things
take the time they take, you know. But I felt a lot more comfortable,
less stuck in old guilty feelings, after I let the old habits go."*

19.

Don't look for help where it isn't available.

ॐ   ॐ   ॐ

In the face of an obstacle which is impossible to overcome, stubbornness is stupid.

—SIMONE DE BEAUVOIR

It's always easier to proceed with what you believe is right when the people who matter to you agree with what you are doing.

Not all of those people are going to agree with the plans and decisions you make when you are getting divorced. In some cases, you may hold those friends and relatives in such high esteem or feel so dependent upon them that their negative response to your situation feels crushing. How can you go on without their understanding and approval?

Now is the time to rely on the courage of your convictions. You will not be able to make everyone in your life understand or support your position. Not everyone can be fair or rational in the face of such an emotional event.

Sometimes parents and in-laws have a difficult time accepting the end of their children's marriage. Other relatives and friends who have counted on you as a couple may also bring their own baggage along when they try to deal with this change in your life.

It's hard to walk away feeling misunderstood and unsupported by people who are significant to you, yet you cannot compel them to see things your way. The best thing you can do is to simply state your views clearly to them, let them know that their support and understanding are important to you, and leave them alone to think things through.

In time, some of them will probably begin to see things differently and will let you know that they want to help. Others may not be able to take up with you where they left off. You will not be able to count on them as you once did.

You *can* count on many other people in your life, no doubt. If you need to talk things out, or cry things out, why knock on a closed door when other doors will be flung wide open for you as soon as you ask? You cannot get what you want from whom you want when you want. But you can usually get what you want if you look for where it's available.

- No one can control, or always accurately predict, the opinions of others.
- The only one you must justify yourself to is yourself.
- Look for flowers in the field where you see them growing, not in the empty field.

"For years now I've depended on my friend Maura for advice," says Rennie, 34. *"We both work in marketing. She has loads of experience and she has been very important in guiding my career. I separated from my husband two years ago and when I told Maura what was going on she just didn't have much to say. I'd tell her a long, sad story and she would say something sort of noncommittal and then change the subject. I wouldn't say that we were close personal friends. Our friendship was based more on our business relationship. But my life was so topsy-turvy that I couldn't help talking about what was going on, and I did think that Maura would, as always, have some good advice. One day she simply said to me, 'I'm sorry, Rennie, but I don't believe in divorce. I'm sure you have good reasons for going through with this but I'm not comfortable talking about it.' I felt stung by that and I stopped calling her to have lunch. I found other people I could talk to who were very sympathetic and helpful to me. But, to*

her credit, Maura hung in there. She kept calling me for lunch, even after I'd turned her down a couple of times, so we continued to see each other. We just didn't talk about my divorce. Now that I don't need to talk about it quite so much, or feel so raw, that isn't a problem. And I realized that Maura was just doing what I've always counted on her to do with me—playing it straight. Not every friendship suits every area of your life. Probably most don't."

20.

Start a new social life for yourself.

ৡ ৡ ৡ

Variety is the soul of pleasure.
—Aphra Behn

When is the right time to get a new social life underway for yourself? As soon as you feel up to it.

But how in the world do you go about doing that? By doing what comes naturally to you.

Your new social life will start as soon as you put yourself out in the world. Its terms are also up to you. If you are more comfortable going out for the evening with one or more other women, invite some friends to go out with you. If you'd rather go to a lecture or a movie alone, go. If you want to meet men, go to places and events where you are likely to enjoy yourself, and to meet people who share your interests.

In the early weeks of separation, some women feel suddenly free and ready to go out as much as possible. Others feel vulnerable and exposed, and lean toward staying close to home where it feels safe. Those who were married for many years may feel that their single social skills are rusty. How do you meet people? How do you talk to them?

It doesn't have to be hard. In fact, the easier you make it for yourself, the more successful it is likely to be for you.

Get yourself out among people you enjoy who are doing activities you enjoy. Don't wait for friends to come knocking on your door. Be bold. You probably have more time now to develop new friendships with people you have met at work or in other areas of your life. Get a couple of tickets to the next concert that appeals to you and ask a potential new friend to go with you. You'll probably find a lot of single women who have the time and enthusiasm to try something new that looks like a good time.

You might have to push yourself at first, to get over shyness or feeling not up to company. It's important to push yourself. Getting out among people is a healthy move. You need to put yourself in the world now.

And when you're out there having a good time, you'll be attractive to other people. As everybody's mother likes to say, "Just go, have a good time. Who knows? You might meet somebody nice."

- Tell yourself that at least twice a month you will make plans to go out with a friend, or to a group social event.

- Choose activities and places that are genuinely appealing to you, especially some you've never tried before. Why not?

- Your only goal right now is the experience of a pleasant evening or a pleasant day spent among other people.

"My ex-husband had me so brainwashed by the time our relationship came to an end that I truly believed I would never ever have a relationship with a man again," says Carla, who was thirty-eight and the mother of three at the time of her divorce. "I didn't even think about it. I tried to find a woman's group for people who had recently separated. My marriage had been in such bad shape for so long that I had pushed everyone away, so that at the worst time, I couldn't even make a phone call to anyone. I was no one. I felt so isolated it was horrible. Don't ever do that. Men come and go, but the women stay. Those are the folks I hang onto in real life . . . So I tried a couple of groups and everyone was talking about how to meet men. I was so much not there, and I kept thinking what is wrong with me? I didn't fit in anywhere. Finally I did find a group that really kind of got me where I wanted to go. It was a group of ten or twelve divorced women.

At one point I remember saying to one of them, 'You know, I think I would like to meet somebody and I think if I sit here in this house like this, nobody's going to fall through the ceiling into my lap.' So I started to go to some of these singles things, which was very difficult at first, with my new women friends dragging me kicking and screaming. And that's how it began. At some point I decided that I really needed to take care of myself, so I started to go out and meet people. And I had fun, so I kept going."

21.

Negotiate your new relationship with your old friends.

ॐ ॐ ॐ

Intimacy is a difficult art.
—VIRGINIA WOOLF

Suddenly you wake up one day and you've lost your escort. Your duo has gone mono. You're yin without yang. Friends are unsure how to issue invitations to you now: Do your married friends ask you alone to dinner or a movie now? Or should they wait until you can bring a date or until they can find one for you?

Some of them will stop asking you to go out at all. Some women will invite your company only in the daytime, saving evenings for "couples" time.

Those friends who don't assume you turned in your "Certified Independent Adult" license when you separated may continue to ask you to go out with them as always. But you are likely to feel awkward being a third or fifth wheel for the evening. How should you handle it?

For one thing, pay your own way. If you make it clear that you enjoy the company of your friends, that you would like more evenings out with them, and that you expect to hold up your end of the deal as always, they are likely to arrange evenings with you more often.

Reciprocate. There's no reason why you can't have friends over for brunch or dinner, if that's something you enjoy. Why should you need a date to help you make a barbecue?

Mix old friends and new friends together. Your oldest friend-ships might be enlivened by bringing those friends together with the new, single friends you are making now. Don't feel that you have to segregate the people from your married life from the peo-ple you meet as a newly single woman.

If someone you really like has stopped calling since your sepa-ration, call him or her yourself. They may simply feel uncertain about how to get together with you now. Go first. Show the way. And if that doesn't work, let it go and make arrangements with people who have already proved themselves to be reliable com-panions.

- Don't wait for friends to make the first move. Show them that you are eager to continue your relationship to them.

- If you are in the company of good friends, you can get past awkwardness and learn to feel comfortable with being unes-corted at a social event.

- Don't split your life between old friends and new. Invite people from each group to get together to give yourself more sense of continuity.

"After I'd been separated for several months," says Anne Marie, 33, "my old friends Jan and Mark asked me if I wanted to go hear some jazz with them. We all used to like a particular group that came to town now and then, and they were coming to a club we like that weekend. I was delighted, and really glad that they didn't hesitate to ask me. So we all went—it turned out they had asked another woman to come too. She was a divorced friend of theirs I had met before. I had a really terrific time. It felt so good to get out to a place I wouldn't have gone to by myself, and to be with Jan and Mark. When the check came, Mark just scooped it up and handed back his credit card. I tried to pay him for my part but he wouldn't take it, and the other woman wasn't making any attempt, so I quit and just said thank you very

much. But that night I wrote Mark a note and put a check in with it. I said that I had had a wonderful time, and that I wanted to feel free to propose another evening out together without feeling that I was going to burden them with paying my way, especially when that wasn't necessary. I thanked him and Jan for being such great friends. When I saw Mark again he said that had been really helpful to him in letting him see how he could best stick by me. So we all do go out more, and I feel just fine about it."

22.

Define your new role with your former mate.

❧ ❧ ❧

The one with the primary responsibility to the individual's future is that individual.

—DORCAS HARDY

Whatever role you played in your marriage, you now have a new part to play. The bad news is that you will probably be playing this part without consistent cooperation from your fellow players. The good news is that you get to direct your own part.

When it comes to emotional situations, many women are in the habit of placing themselves in a position to react rather than to act. In every phase of divorce it is important to remember that you probably have more power and leverage than you think. If you do not try to watch for opportunities to jump into the driver's seat, you will wind up on someone else's trip.

You probably know your former mate quite well. Now you must use that knowledge to help define what your new role with him will be. If he is a hothead, and certain topics or behaviors of yours have always set him off, you are sure to make more trouble for yourself by plunging into those areas without a strategy.

If he wants to see you a lot to discuss whatever matters are of mutual concern, but you wish to see less of him, see less of him. You will not gain any ground by letting him define the terms of your new relationship.

Just as you cannot live his life for him, just as you must learn to let go of any overcharged sense of responsibility for his well-being or happiness, you must learn not to count on him to share your goals or even to care about them.

Therefore, it is important for you to give yourself the part you want to play. What the other players do in response to that is up to them. If you don't want to get into shouting matches every time you talk, don't shout. If he shouts, that's his problem. Sooner or later, the fact that you are no longer playing the old part—the one that apparently didn't work very well—is bound to have an effect. It's hard to stage a sword fight if only one person on stage is willing to pick up a sword.

Be practical. Being right is sometimes less important than getting done what you want to get done. Take a keen look at what kind of practical, harmonious relationship is possible and desirable with your former mate. Now what steps can you take to accomplish that goal without compromising your newfound autonomy and self-respect?

- You are no longer playing the role you played in your marriage.
- You will make more progress toward your goals if you *plan* your dealings with your former mate.
- Be true to yourself: Don't let your former mate direct your part.

"In every area apart from money, we had pretty civil communication," says Peggy, 51. She and Harry were married for fourteen years and had two children. *"There were years of keeping track of the kids, when one of them would break curfew and I'd call Harry and say, 'Harry, have you heard from Michelle?' And he'd willingly help make calls to her friends or whatever we needed to do until she came home. But I really had to learn who my audience was with him. There were certain things he did that pushed certain buttons for me always and then we would get into fights. But as time went on I became much*

more pragmatic and I became much more conscious of the fact that my buttons were going to be pushed, so I'd think about it. I'd think, well, you need to get this accomplished, and in order to get this accomplished you need to talk to him in this way. He's a person who when he pours juice into two glasses, he measures them so that they are exactly equal, so no one gets more than anyone else. So, I put aside the sort of reasoning I would have used with my friends and I tried to arrange things so that he would feel that everything we shared was shared fifty-fifty. When my daughter graduated, I wanted us to participate equally. So she had lunch with his family, she had dinner with my family. Her time was split equally between the two families, and yet he was upset because he felt that he wasn't getting an even amount. So the next time when my son graduated, I said 'Why don't you just tell Dad that you're going to have all the dinners with him and he'll think that dinners are more important than lunches.' And sure enough, everything went absolutely smoothly. I've been doing a lot of that. I have to know who I'm dealing with and I have to play into that. I can't just say 'I'm going to do this because it is right,' because that doesn't work. I have to be more pragmatic than that."

23.

Face facts: No one with children ever really gets divorced.

৶ ৶ ৶

Sharing is sometimes more demanding than giving.
—MARY CATHERINE BATESON

If you and your former mate have children together, you will continue to have a relationship with each other as long as you are parents. Whether it is a good, working relationship will be up to both of you. You must continue to work together on this issue. Neither of you can make it work alone.

Even if you take full custody of your children, move halfway across the country as a result of your divorce, and eventually remarry, your children's father will remain their father. If he is a non-presence or a troubling presence in their lives, your relationship will be one of feeling, and perhaps resenting, his absence or his troublemaking.

Even when you have little contact with each other, occasions will arise often enough to summon both parents to play traditional roles. Birthdays, holidays, graduations, special honors, weddings, bar and bat mitzvahs, christenings, and so on roll around more frequently than you might imagine. And when they do, if both parents haven't resolved the roles they will play, the pain of having dismantled the family will be reawakened.

The healthiest course for everyone is for parents to remain in at least cordial contact with each other, if not close cooperation. When you imagine your future, take time to imagine the kind of relationship you would most like to have with your children's father. What steps can you take to assure that that is, in fact, the relationship that you will have?

He will have to do his part, too, and you may not be able to work out exactly the relationship you would like to have. But it is important to realize that you cannot wish him away, or wish away the occasions when you must continue to share a parenting role with him. Put your energy instead toward making your continuing parenting relationship one that you can live with, gracefully if possible. Try to do your part to take anxiety and awkwardness out of family occasions. That will be a gift to your children, as well as to yourself.

- Even when our children have children of their own, we are still their parents.
- Be a good role model for your children by aiming for a good working relationship with their father.
- Put the children's needs in this area ahead of your own.

"Ed and I were just too young when we got married," says Connie, 46. "We had children when we were scarcely into our twenties. The strain of taking all that on too young broke us up after seven years, and Ed took off to sow his oats, I guess, leaving me with the two boys. We all always knew that he cared for the boys, but sometimes months would go by without our hearing from him and he wasn't always responsible about paying his child support. I've probably let a lot of my worst memories and feelings about that get lost by now, because my sons are both out of college now, so that was a long time ago. But I do know that I never wanted to keep the boys from Ed, or to get in the way of what fathering he was able to offer them when he did come around. And after a few years he seemed to begin to take stock of things, and to be able to give more to the boys. He began to take them with him on trips, and he moved back to the town where we lived so he could see more of them. I had remarried and had a daughter by

then. We all get along all right. The boys still need all of us, too. Ed and I are sharing the cost of health insurance for one of them, and we chipped in on a used car for the other. We don't talk about anything but the kids, really, but it's good that we can talk about these things and do them together, because it feels better. To me, I know, and probably to all of us."

24.

Speak kindly of your former mate, but don't lie to your children.

❧ ❧ ❧

Kind words can be short and easy to speak, but their echoes are truly endless.

—MOTHER TERESA

Most parents want their children to be self-confident and supported by loving family relationships. Divorce is a blow to both of these objectives. But the effect of divorce on your children can be managed and its negative impact kept to a minimum if you can remember to let your head rule your heart.

It's difficult to resist rallying your troops when your former mate is behaving like a creep. You may want to beat your breast and yell from the rooftops that he has once again failed to send the support check on time, or that he's reneged on a promise to switch a child-care weekend with you. But just as you wouldn't want your neighbors to see you in that state of mind, you shouldn't come apart all over your children either. Buy a punching bag. This too shall pass.

If your children ask what's bothering you, tell them as much of the true story as you feel it is in their best interest to know. You can say "Money is tight this month," without blaming anyone for it. You can say that you hope you can find a good babysitter for Saturday night, without adding that it was their father's turn to be with them and thus risk their feeling unwanted by either of you.

No child, not even an adult child, wants to hear his or her parent judged, criticized, or ridiculed, least of all by the other parent. Children need to be allowed to come to terms with the significant relationships in their lives and to make the most of them. Unless your former mate is a danger to them, you will do your best for your children by giving them room to create their own relationship with their father, and to come to their own conclusions about his strengths and weaknesses.

The differences you have with your former mate are between you and him; not you, him, and the kids. Even if what makes you the most angry is his failure to do what you think is right for your children, that is an issue between you and him, not an issue for the children to be involved in.

Your children will be confused, and perhaps alienated, by being forced to choose sides. If they are allowed to decide for themselves how they want to relate to each of their parents, they may surprise you with the wisdom of their perceptions and choices. Furthermore, they are more likely to open up to you and tell you what troubles them, and allow you to help them work out their feelings, if they don't have to fear that any mention of a problem will launch a tirade from you.

- Respect your children's ability to figure things out for themselves.
- Keep the big picture in mind. You may not always be so angry.
- Keep your children's need for two loving parents always in mind.

"There were days," says Sandy, "when I would almost have wanted to take out a contract on Greg. He didn't send child support for over a year. He took off for England for a month without telling me. He was unbelievably outrageous." Sandy and Greg were divorced after

thirteen years of marriage, when their children were nine and three years old. "I wanted to tell my son that his father didn't love him enough to care whether we could pay the rent, or to let him know he'd be gone for a while. Sometimes I did say that kind of thing and I'd get a look at the kids' faces and I'd feel like a toad. It just didn't help anything. I felt just as frustrated afterward, and I felt like a bad mom on top of it. The little changes Greg has made in his behavior, and believe me, he is not a model parent, are improvements. I try now to praise every good thing he does for the kids, accentuate the positive, because I want them to feel proud, not rejected. And maybe I can encourage Greg to do more."

25.

Be a mother, not a martyr.

❧ ❧ ❧

When my mother had to get dinner for eight she'd just make enough for sixteen and only serve half.
—GRACIE ALLEN

No one is well served by a martyr. Martyrs give up what they really want or need. And those for whom they make their great sacrifices are saddled with guilt, and denied the pleasure of giving in return. Giving is a two-way street. Love cannot mature and grow to its fullest potential if it remains a one-way proposition, if it goes only in one direction, from me to you. Real love allows for reciprocation, so that those we love can double their pleasure by giving to us as we give to them.

Yet, as mothers, we are often tempted to give up what matters to us in order to give our most or our best to our children. Particularly when we believe our children are suffering, we leap to bridge the gap.

It's true that children suffer in divorce. Although there is much you can do to smooth the way for your children, you cannot make everything all right. And if you give up too much that matters to you, you risk making everything all wrong.

If a five-year-old feels proud of setting the dinner table, why would anyone try to "spare" him this chore? If you spare your children from making sacrifices for your family, from working toward common goals with you, you will deny them the important reward of feeling that their deeds and words are significant not only to themselves but to those they care for.

If your teenager wants a concert ticket that costs forty dollars, she might enjoy the concert twice as much if she has worked to pay for the ticket herself, especially if you would have had to give something up yourself to buy it for her.

If Mother's Day falls on a day when your children would normally be with their father, ask him to make a trade with you. Let your children know that you appreciate signs of care from them, that they matter to you. They will find far more pride and comfort in that than they would in being told that it really doesn't matter. It matters. *You* matter. Don't be afraid to say so.

- ꙮ Don't be afraid to claim what is important to you.
- ꙮ Allow your children the pleasure of *giving* to you, not only the pleasure of receiving.
- ꙮ Love is a two-way street. It just comes to a dead end if it only goes one way.

Overcompensating is an easy pitfall for parents. Sarah, now fifty-three, left her husband of eighteen years when her daughters were fourteen and thirteen. The children remained with their father. "When I separated from my husband, and because I had had to leave my kids with him," Sarah says, "I wanted desperately to prove that I was a good mother, to prove that I loved them. If they called at any time of the day or night, if I had any plans, if I had a date, I dropped everything for them. I wanted to compensate for this horrible, fatal flaw, this crime that I had committed. In retrospect, it did both of them a terrible disservice. I never demonstrated any self-respect to them. So, in ten years, I had my kids with me for one Thanksgiving. That was painful. No Christmases, no Easters. One Thanksgiving. I never said to them 'This hurts my feelings. I want you with me.' I didn't want to anger their father. I tried to do whatever would be easier for them. I hurt myself and them because they came to understand that I had such low standards for their responsibilities toward me. Even now I have a difficult time saying, 'I need you to be with me.' I would do so much differently now, but I don't beat myself over the head with it. I was a different person then. The best thing that I could have done was to say to them, 'I left for good reasons, I'm entitled to a life, I'll be the best mother I can be but not at my own expense.' Now that is exactly what I say. I let them know that I want their love and attention just as much as they want mine. And even though they are young adults now, it is still very important for all three of us."

26.

Answer your children's questions.

ᕙ ᕙ ᕙ

Truth, like surgery, may hurt, but it cures.
—Han Suyin

Especially if you have teenagers you may soon get the "why exactly are you getting divorced?" questions. It's important to take these questions seriously when they come up and not to brush them aside with a pat response.

Avoiding your children's questions will be unsettling to them and will create problems in the whole complex of your communication with them. Now is the time to keep communication as open as you can—that's the best sort of support you can give your children, and it will help you, too. Try to make your answers as complete and truthful as possible, but leave out the kind of personal details that might be painful for a child. Your children are entitled to a truthful answer to their questions, but not necessarily to the whole story of your marriage and divorce.

Don't try to answer questions for their father. Send those to him. Don't even speculate about what he might say. Your children must be allowed to work out their own relationship with their father. Respect their privacy and try to refrain from asking them what their father said.

If your children don't seem to have many questions they are probably just having difficulty asking them. Do your part to create openings in your conversations with them that might encourage them to voice their concerns. Children are often shy about bringing up painful subjects. In this case, they know that it may be painful for you as well as for them, so their inhibition may be extreme. Let them know, with as much subtlety as possible, that you are open to their questions, that you hope they will express whatever fears and anxieties they may be feeling.

Don't push them to talk past the point when they are satisfied, or made uncomfortable, by your answers. Here is another area where patience is a virtue. The questions in their minds that surround your divorce are probably many and complicated. Their questioning may go on for years, and they may need to hear some things over and over again before they can fully take in the information they receive.

You have a lifetime of dialogue with your children ahead of you. If they feel safe and well regarded in the way you answer their questions, that dialogue is likely to be continuous and rewarding for all of you.

- Try to take time to answer your children's questions carefully, even if they ask them just when you are most exhausted or pressed for time.
- Don't try to answer questions for which you don't have answers. Be honest.
- Be guided in your answers by your care for your children rather than by your personal feelings about your divorce.

"The other day," says Judy, 48, *"my fifteen-year-old son was telling me about the mother of one of his friends whose husband had died recently. It was her fiftieth birthday, so her son and his buddies all took her out for dinner. And Eric said, 'It's really sad. She's fifty now and she's totally by herself.' And I said, 'Well, I'm almost fifty and I'm by myself,' and Eric shot back, 'Yeah, but you chose to be by yourself.' Then I realized how angry he still is, a year after our divorce. He said, 'If things were so bad with you and Dad, why'd you wait twenty years to get divorced? Do you really think things are better now?' So I took a deep breath and I told him that as hard as it's been,*

the last two years, with all their problems, are an improvement over the life I had before. All I have to do is think of the silent dinners we had every single night for twenty years and these past two years seem like a piece of cake. I don't usually say stuff like that to Eric, but I felt like I had to level with him. I said that the relationship that he had with his dad and the one that I had had were very different. The fact that his father and I were unhappy did not mean that his father wasn't a good person or that he and his father shouldn't have a good, close relationship. I can't pretend I'm not glad I finally found the courage to get out of my marriage. I don't think that would be helpful anyway. I don't complain about his dad to Eric, or ask him to share my feelings, but I think kids need to hear about your real feelings so that they don't harbor the notion that you're going to get back together, or so that they don't have to feel so excluded from your inner life. I wouldn't tell Eric all my thoughts, not by any means. But he's old enough to deal with the basic outline. Later on he told me he respected my honesty, if not all of my decisions. Hey, coming from a teenager, I think that's high praise! Our understanding of each other seems to be increasing, in spite of our disagreements."

27.

Listen to your children.

We want people to feel with us more than to act for us.
—GEORGE ELIOT

The most loving and useful thing you can do for your children right now, and always, is to listen to them. As overburdened as you probably are by going through this transition, your effort to stop and listen to your children whenever they try to talk to you will be rewarding in important and lasting ways.

Being heard is being healed. Even if what the kids are talking about seems trivial, or repetitious, your active listening to them applies balm to their souls.

Casual conversations that begin in a relaxed atmosphere can often lead to important discussions in which you find out what's really on your child's mind.

If you keep the habit of listening with real attention when your younger children tell you about their day or what they saw on TV, you are establishing a pattern that may even help overcome some of the natural reticence of teenagers later on in their lives.

Listening does not mean interrupting to offer solutions to problems. Some subtle guidance that can help your children get to their own solutions will be much, much more useful, and less likely to bring the conversation to a sudden stop.

Even a child who asks for attention by screaming and yelling can calm down surprisingly quickly if she is not argued with or told to calm down, but is simply heard for a few minutes.

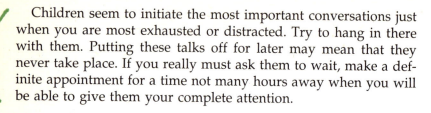

Children seem to initiate the most important conversations just when you are most exhausted or distracted. Try to hang in there with them. Putting these talks off for later may mean that they never take place. If you really must ask them to wait, make a definite appointment for a time not many hours away when you will be able to give them your complete attention.

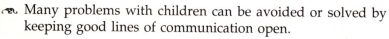

- ✐ Many problems with children can be avoided or solved by keeping good lines of communication open.
- ✐ You will learn more about what your children are thinking if you refrain from contradicting their points of view.
- ✐ Good listening is good loving.

"I have two sons and a daughter," says Sheila, 46. "One of my sons never talked about his feelings about the divorce; the other one did. I had read an article about boys and how boys react to divorce and I just brought that up one day in order to get him to talk. I said, 'Gee, I read this interesting article about boys and divorce. It said it takes boys a longer time to get over it even though they don't initially react.' And he thought about it and he said, 'I actually feel good, because I think it's the most difficult thing I've ever gone through and I think I've gone through it real well and I think I feel stronger for it.' And then he said, 'I used to lie awake at night and try to picture all the rooms in our old house one by one, and try to remember every detail in each room. It got harder to be sure I was remembering them the way they really were. And after that I could see that I used to make myself feel sad when I did that, but that it didn't make me sad anymore. It wasn't that interesting anymore.' He had never, ever talked about the old house before, and neither had the other kids. I didn't say anything when he told me that because I was a little choked up. Then he said, 'I never wanted to tell anyone how I felt about that before.' So, wow! This was an occasion, him telling me that. I was so glad I took that time to have a leisurely conversation that day, and just to hear him."

28.

Start new family traditions.

❧ ❧ ❧

To be rooted is perhaps the most important and least recognized need of the human soul.
—SIMONE WEIL

Some of the strong, essential threads in the fabric of life are our traditions. The sprinkling of holidays across the calendar gives us a regular opportunity to gather together year after year with the people who are important to us, to remind ourselves of those relationships and our pleasure in sharing life with each other. The unique ways in which your family celebrates birthdays, the beach cottage you return to every summer, are reminders of what you can rely on; they help make you feel safe and cared for.

Obviously, divorce interrupts those patterns. Holidays and special occasions suddenly can become painfully lonely times that remind you that everything has changed. In some instances, they can even become battlefields where former mates go to war over who gets custody of friends and relatives for Thanksgiving. Warm rooms can turn icy cold when both husband and wife attempt to attend the same traditional Christmas dinner before their differences have been sufficiently resolved.

It doesn't have to be like that.

For most people, the best approach is not to try to keep things the same, but to take a step in the opposite direction. If you are accustomed to going to your in-laws for Thanksgiving, try making Thanksgiving dinner yourself this year. Invite some friends and relatives who have not celebrated that holiday with you before, to make sure the atmosphere will be really fresh, rather than imitative of something out of the past. If you and your children have always spent a week at the beach in the summer, try the mountains, or try a different beach. Ask another family with children if they would like to try a new vacation spot with you.

As a rule, children do not like change. They will balk at any suggestions you make about changing the family vacation habits or doing Thanksgiving differently. You'll have an easier time with them if you think through your proposals before telling them what you plan to do. Let them help with planning some of the details, but be firm about your intention not to do things the old way.

If you can create an adventure, or even a new recipe, instead of giving in to missing the way things were, you are likely to add to your feelings of pride and accomplishment, and to have a better time. The traditions of the past are not gone. You are simply adding to them. Soon, when some of these occasions turn out to be great fun, you will find that you have new traditions to treasure.

- You won't miss the old so much if you make something new.
- Invite some new people to make new traditions with you.
- Don't let holidays sneak up on you. Make plans.

"Maybe it's easier to be flexible without children," says Chris, 39. "For the first two years after Todd and I split I tried different things at Christmas. I tried visiting my family on the West Coast, which was not a good thing. They were still trying to figure out how they felt about my pending divorce and it was very hard for me to relax there. The next year I tried an aunt and uncle who live just a couple of hours away, but their Christmas was so radically different from the kinds of Christmases I was used to that I felt like I was participating in a foreign holiday. So what I started to do is to take the advice of friends. Last year I went with a friend to go skiing in a remote area that she knew well. This little town had all kinds of holiday celebrations. The

whole town turned out for a huge bonfire, with people all around and singing. All the bars and restaurants were very festive. I met all kinds of people from other states and had a terrific time getting to know them. It was a lovely, special time. It was so refreshing. I came back feeling I hadn't had to deal with any craziness. I was gone only six days. Even three would have been enough. It was worth what it cost, too. Even if I'd just gone to a little mountain cabin nearby and had just eaten good meals and walked in the forest, it would have been sufficient, and better than trying to cobble together a holiday based on other people's traditions. I don't know whether it will be a permanent tradition, but it was great. It was in its own way very spiritual. And celebratory."

29.

Don't let your children choose your dates.

℞ ℞ ℞

One half of the world cannot understand the pleasures of the other.

—JANE AUSTEN

Yes, single mothers can have a social life. Even in a house full of children, there must be room for you and your needs.

Going out with a group of friends is not so hard. Your children are probably used to seeing you go out with other adults. But what about the first time a strange man comes to the house to take you out for the evening? Should he even come to the house at all?

You will have to decide on your own ground rules for dating. Things are likely to go more smoothly if you stop to look at how your children are doing with the idea of your being a single woman. Their readiness to accept the idea of your having new men in your life will have to do not only with their ages but with how safe each of them feels with that concept, and how far they have come in the process of accepting your separation and divorce.

Children act out their feelings in different ways. If you think that your children are behaving oddly or destructively around the issue of your having male friends, or if you feel puzzled about how best to mesh your need for a social life with their need for security, you might consult a professional counselor, one who specializes in children, for advice. You can get a lot of help in just an hour or two with the right person.

Talk to your children yourself. Tell them what your plans are for the weekend. They will feel safer if they know what you are doing than they will feel if you try to go off without telling them anything. Even if you limit your dates to weekends when the children are not with you, let them know that you have been going out.

You can take your cues about how much to say, how soon to introduce a new man to them from your children themselves. But it is not good for you or for them to allow their objections to a particular person or to the whole idea of your going out to dominate what you do. Children really do not want that kind of power over you. Even in their struggles with you over issues like this, they want you to win. Be firm about your right to choose your own friends. And be generous about their right not to agree with your choices. That way, all of you will have the freedom you need to see your choices clearly.

- ∽ You and your children all need time to adjust to your new social life. Don't rush things.
- ∽ Don't dictate your children's feelings any more than you would allow them to dictate yours.
- ∽ Be the adult. Don't give your children more power than a child can handle.

"Men would come to my house to pick me up and my kids would disappear," says Phyllis, 52. "They'd go into the basement and disappear. It was important to me to let them do that. I never introduced my children to any man who walked in, never asked them to be polite. I mean, I didn't want them to be obnoxious and awful, but they didn't have to be friendly or come up out of the basement. If they didn't want to deal with it, if they wanted to keep as far away from it as possible, that was fine. I didn't say to a man, 'Let's go out and let's bring my children.' Never, never. When I finally decided that my kids were going

to do something with a man, or he was going to come over to dinner, it was a big deal. My dates knew there were kids because the place was always a wreck, but I didn't put any pressure on the kids. I know a lot of people would say, 'Johnny, show Sam your room.' But my kids weren't comfortable with it, and that was fine. At one point my daughter, who was an adolescent, informed me that she didn't like Man X, but she really liked Man Y and that she was mad and wasn't going to talk to me or him if this one came versus that one. That was good because then I said to her, 'Look, this is my life and these are my choices, and if you want to be angry about it, that's your choice. I'm an adult and I deserve a relationship and I don't tell you who your friends should be.' She never said another word about it. I think she was just testing the waters. It might have been easy to say, 'Oh my God, she doesn't like him, and what's going to happen if we have a serious relationship?' But I didn't do that. And this happened to be the man I married ten years ago. And they get along just fine. I think she really accepted that, that I was allowed to have a life of my own.''

30.

Support your former mate's relationship with your children.

❧ ❧ ❧

We are rich only through what we give, and poor only through what we refuse.

—ANNE-SOPHIE SWETCHINE

Your children have two parents. That is as true today as it was yesterday and will be tomorrow. Because you care about them, it is in your best interest to support their relationship with their father, whatever form it takes, and regardless of your own relationship with him.

You can be supportive of that relationship without being involved in it. Begin by honoring whatever terms you have agreed to about where and when the children see their father. If you have agreed to have them ready to be picked up at six o'clock every Thursday, see that they are ready by 5:55. If you have agreed that the children may go on vacation with their father for a month in the summer, don't look for reasons why this won't work or is not convenient. Help make it work, even if it isn't convenient.

In the long run, it will be better for you to cooperate in seeing that your children have calm, easy access to time with their father than it would be for you to try to place a lot of restrictions around that time.

Make it easy for them to have frequent contact. Encourage them to speak with their father by phone as often as they want to, and allow them privacy in those conversations. Their confidence in both their parents will grow if they are allowed the freedom to relate to each of you the way they want to.

While you should insist that your former mate be considerate of you, your schedule, and your house rules, try not to get too upset about little things. If he brings the children back to your house an hour late, a calm reminder that your time and your peace of mind must be respected and that you would like to be informed if he expects to be late is likely to produce better results for you than would running out to his car and yelling that he's late again.

Share with their father information about the children that comes to you via their schools, the pediatrician, or their babysitters, especially when it is information that will be useful to his relationship with them. Ask him to let you know, too, about things he learns in his time with the children. If the children know that the two of you have open communication about them, they are less likely to try, as kids will, to play you off against each other, a tactic that isn't good for anyone. Even if you have difficulty talking to your former mate right now, you can always write notes. And that may even lead to your growing more comfortable with talking to each other—a worthwhile goal.

- Expect your children's father to respect your rules and schedules, but don't place arbitrary restrictions on his time with the children.
- Allow your children liberal use of the telephone to help support their relationship with their father.
- When you take pictures at a school play or a basketball tournament, have duplicates made and pass them on.

"Don and I share custody of the children. When we agreed to that I really didn't think too much about what sharing meant, other than in the time and physical sense of it," says Natalie, 45. *"We seem to have worked out our routines with the kids pretty easily, probably because we get along well and haven't felt like we had to prove any-*

thing to each other. We both go to school events, and now each of us brings our new person along and we are all fine about that. The kids know they can't dodge things by using one of us either, because we talk about what goes on. My fourteen-year-old son had some friends to my house when I wasn't home one night recently. I don't allow the kids to have friends in when I'm not home, and he knew I was going to come down on him when I found out. So he went to his dad's that Monday after school instead of being with me, where he was supposed to be. Usually I don't make a big deal if the kids have some reason to want some extra time with their dad. They're old enough to choose. But I called Don and told him what was going on, and he drove Alex back to my house right away so Alex would have to face the music. I would have done the same thing if Alex had done something at Don's and tried to hide out from it. I think it would be hard to raise these guys if the two of us didn't uphold each other's house rules and rights with the kids.''

31.

Don't try to supervise your former mate's parenting.

ᘓ ᘓ ᘓ

More children suffer from interference than from non-interference.

—AGATHA CHRISTIE

Your former husband is probably going to be the same kind of parent he was during your marriage. Once the dust settles after you separate, you are likely to find that whatever you admired about his parenting is intact. Likewise, whatever was problematical between you is likely to continue to be problematical now.

When you are separated or divorced, you have less reason and less opportunity to work out the differences in your parenting philosophies. You can help prevent problems from growing between the two of you by accepting the differences in your styles and values, as long as no real harm is being done to the children. Naturally, you need to feel confident that the children's health and safety are not being endangered.

Do your best to focus on the good that comes of their father's parenting, and to absorb the minor conflicts that are more irritating than harmful. If he lets the children stay up later than you do, but their health and their grades don't seem to show any ill effects, don't make an issue of it. Let the children adjust to the change in time zones between your homes. If he lets them eat more junk food than you do, you must decide whether that's worth arguing about.

When you do have issues that seem significant, try to discuss them with him, rather than to insist that he follow your rules and methods. If you find that the children are not getting their homework done when they are at their father's house, tell him that you have noticed the problem and give him the opportunity to come up with a solution to it. Don't tell him what to do. If you discover that the children are afraid of his temper, tell him about that too— but tell, don't yell. Give him the chance to resolve problems his way. The more you can stay clear of a power struggle over parenting, the more the children will benefit.

- In many daily respects, you and your former mate are no longer co-parents. You are independent, but you can and should be cooperative with each other.
- Making an issue over petty differences may cause major difficulties.
- Let go of your desire to control your former mate's parenting and focus on its good points.

"My son is seven. His dad and I stopped living together when Jason was three and a half," says Allison, 38. *"Jason lives with me and spends every other weekend with his father. If they want to stay up until eleven o'clock at night and watch PG-13-rated videos all weekend, at least it only happens every other weekend. It is no longer my business. Charles is his parent, too, and even if his standards are not mine, I'll have to live with them. At first, I went into this so naively. I thought I really wanted this ex-husband of mine, who was a problematical father while he was living with me, to be a real dad, not just a weekend dad. So Jason used to be with his dad every Thursday through Sunday. I thought that would mean he'd be involved in his life, he wouldn't just be some kind of Disney World dad on the weekends. But for many complicated reasons, that arrangement didn't work out. So now, eventually, after a lot of court battles we're back to every other weekend. And I think that's fine. Let Jason grow up with his dad being a Disney World dad. That's the contribution he has to make to*

him right now. It's not my place to try to push it further, into some-thing it probably can't be. And if it changes and gets better, I'll be thrilled. Jason will reach his own conclusions as he grows up. My main job here is to try to keep the daily routines as easy as I can for him."

32.

Trust your children to work things out for themselves.

❧ ❧ ❧

Those who trust us, educate us.
—GEORGE ELIOT

If you think about it, you know it's true that the things we learn best are the things we learn from our own experience.

While you are learning the life lessons of divorce, your children are learning their own lessons. It's difficult to watch them struggle with their feelings, go through anger and depression, and sometimes come to mistaken conclusions. Yet, they must make that journey, just as you must make yours.

Trying to explain things from your point of view will not be much help. Naturally, you want them to understand what has happened, and to agree with your view of events. They are likely to make peace with your divorce sooner, and to come to their own unique conclusions about it, if you let them struggle with it on their own. Don't try to do their thinking for them, no matter how old or how young they are.

What you can do is to show them, and tell them, in as many ways as you can, that you love them and intend to take care of them. Let them know that their feelings are important—and acceptable—to you.

Your children may go through a period of being very angry with you. If they trust you and feel certain that you love them no matter what, they are even more likely to show you how angry they are. That can make you feel terrible. Take heart from knowing that children do not show their true feelings to people they do not trust. Never was it more true than it is true of children that "you always hurt the one you love."

Don't let them abuse you. You don't have to accept their views about you or about the events of your life. You don't have to feel guilty or take responsibility for things that are not your fault. Demand their respect, as you offer them the respect of letting them struggle for themselves. Your belief in their ability to think things through will help them do that.

- ☙ Allow your children time and space to work through their own feelings about your divorce.
- ☙ Let experience speak for itself. Don't try to tell your children what to think.
- ☙ If you show your children that you believe they can think things through for themselves, they will be better equipped to do so.

"One of the most humiliating memories I have is of the first Mother's Day after we separated," says Terry, 46. "My oldest daughter was just eleven then. I knew the kids wouldn't do anything about it and they didn't. I've heard this from many separated women—that their children, especially teenaged children, had not done anything for Mother's Day. It feels to these women like a confirmation that they no longer matter to their kids in the same way. It also gives the children a chance to get revenge for what they've been through. It's very subtle. But this year I got six roses from my three children. They left them on the dining room table. I'd been out of town and when I got back that afternoon, my middle son just pointed to the roses, but didn't say anything. And my youngest son had written a little note that was propped up next to them. It just said, 'These are for you.' Since then I've heard them squabbling among themselves about who hasn't paid his share yet to his sister. I can't tell you how wonderful those roses

made me feel. They did it on their own in their own understated way, and it says to me that they finally feel calm and settled enough to tell me in their way that they love me, and to act like we're still a real family. And we are."

33.

Let your family members work out their own terms with your former mate.

❧ ❧ ❧

Family life! The United Nations is child's play compared to the tugs and splits and need to understand and forgive in any family.

—MAY SARTON

It's always hard to tell the members of your family that you intend to end your marriage. Some people find it's harder to tell their parents that they are separating than it is to tell their own children. Faced with that task, you may find yourself struggling with feelings of having failed, of having let them down.

Your family members—your parents, brothers or sisters, uncles and aunts—each have a history of their own with your former mate, whether or not that history is meaningful to them. Especially if you were married for some length of time, they may have grown very attached to the person who will now no longer be a member of your family. Your separation will be sad news to them, and they will have their own grieving to do.

Of course, you need their support now too. If you feel badly treated by your former mate, you may want your family to line up with you, to join your troops in the battle of divorce.

They may choose to do that. Or they may choose not to. They

may go through phases of their own as they try to come to terms with your divorce. As they work out their own feelings, they may not always be sensitive to yours.

It's important for you to let them know what you want from them. If you want them not to ask you any personal questions about what went wrong, say so. If you are looking to them for a particular kind of help—babysitting, for example, or financial support—say so directly. Be up front about your needs.

At the same time, you must allow them to work out the terms of their parting from, or of their redefining a relationship with, your former spouse. You may wish, at this very moment anyway, never to see him again. But it would be unfair to dictate that your youngest brother, who learned how to drive stick from him, should immediately sever his relationship too.

Even if you try to orchestrate those relationships, you are likely to fail and to feel even worse. As is often the case in your current situation, you will be better off if you focus on what you can do for yourself, and let those around you take care of their own needs.

- Ask for support from your family, but don't try to dictate their behavior toward your former mate.
- Be conscious of your family members' history with your former mate and of how they may be suffering the loss of your marriage along with you.
- If family members are insensitive to your feelings when they try to work out their own feelings about you and your former mate, let them know that you feel hurt. Give them a chance to rethink their attitudes.

"One of the stresses on my marriage was that our jobs had put us into a commuting situation for a couple of years, with no end in sight," says Carrie, 42. *"During the week, my husband stayed with my brother and his wife, because his new job had taken him two hundred miles from where we lived, and where I was working. My brother and my husband became very good friends during that time, and when we*

split up, my brother was extremely upset. Every conversation I had with him ended with him telling me I was making a big mistake and me crying. And my husband was still staying at his house! I felt cheated. I felt like I wanted a big brother to defend me, and instead he was defending my ex-husband. There were a lot of things I could have told him about my ex-husband that might have brought him around to my side, but I didn't want to tell those tales. Essentially, there was nothing to be done about it. We just talked less and less. That was years ago, and over time we have grown closer again, and my ex-husband has moved on with his life and is no longer so attached to my brother. Things between my brother and me are not the same as they were before my divorce, but we have a loving relationship, and I think it's just fine for me not to feel so dependent on my brother. And I'm very glad I never entered into some kind of ugly truth-telling session with him just to vindicate myself. It's not even relevant any-more."

34.

Take charge of your new relationship with your former in-laws.

❧ ❧ ❧

Peace is not won by those who fiercely guard their differences but by those who with open minds and hearts seek out connections.

—KATHERINE PATERSON

There are no formal roles for ex-family members. Given the high rate of divorce, perhaps there will be eventually. But right now, it is up to the members of each family to figure out what their relationship should be to people who are no longer related to them by marriage.

Your former husband's family may need some help in scripting their new relationship with you. If you have had a close relationship with your in-laws and you wish to remain close to them, let them know how you feel. They may be having some trouble sorting out their loyalties. If you show them that you would like to remain close to them without trying to take anything away from their son, you may be able to lead the way to a good continuing relationship with them.

On the other hand, if you have not had much of a relationship with your in-laws, you are unlikely to strengthen it now. You may simply want to do your best to see that their relationship with your children, if you have children, continues with as much contact as all those involved wish to have. If you were the one during your marriage who saw to it that the kids sent cards and gifts at appropriate times, you may now want to leave those tasks to the children's father. Or you may want to carry through on that contact yourself. It's up to you.

Do what comes naturally. Just as you are sorting out your friendships, you can do some sorting of family relationships here too. Family members who are angry with you should be given time to come to their senses and to realize that your divorce is between you and your former husband, that it is neither right nor necessary for them to make a judgment about it. They will have to get over their tribalism if they want to continue to have a good relationship, or any relationship at all, with you.

If members of your former husband's family are people you enjoy and want to stay close to, treat them as you would good friends. Call them up, invite them to do things with you. They may be uncertain about how to relate to you now, and may even feel that you don't want a relationship with them now that your marriage is ending. You need to let them know your feelings about that.

- ❧ Decide for yourself what your ideal relationship with your former in-laws would be. It does not have to be the same with everyone.
- ❧ Let your in-laws know how you would most like to relate to them from now on.
- ❧ Don't get hung up on anyone else's angry behavior. Let them go if they don't behave well toward you.

"I've had more contact with Jeff's family than he's had with mine," says Wendy, 36. *"I've tried to keep contact up, because they live right here in town and I want my daughters to know who all their relatives are and to feel like part of that family. I never had a good relationship with Jeff's mother. We were at odds a lot. I felt like she wanted to tell*

me and my kids what to do all the time, and I'm too headstrong for that. So are the girls! She was divorced herself shortly after we got married and we didn't see much of Jeff's father after that. When it came to our being divorced I had the impression she was supportive of Jeff and glad to be rid of me. But she called me recently about some little thing. It was almost as if she was worried about our losing touch now, so she made up some reason to call. I was very surprised, but I realized right away that it was good that she called. I tried to show her that I'm ready to be friendly with her if we can do it. And I'll call her myself soon, just to return the favor. She's my kids' grandmother. I want them to have all their grandparents in their lives. I want them to have that family history, as long as it's available. As long as we can be friendly and not make each other feel bad, I'm all for it."

35.

Be prepared for some surprising changes in your friendships.

Trouble is a sieve through which we sift our acquaintances. Those too big to pass through are our friends.

—ARLENE FRANCIS

Divorce is a surprisingly public event. You may find that people who wouldn't ordinarily comment on the private matters in your life suddenly feel duty-bound to tell you what they think of your decision, when, of course, you hadn't asked.

Close friends can become harsh critics, finding fault not only with your deciding to divorce but with each step along the way.

Divorce is seen by some people as a frightening threat to the well-being of their community. It's possible that they are afraid their lives, too, might suddenly change without warning. Or perhaps they wish they had the courage to take the steps you are taking.

You may not be able to accurately predict the reaction of each of your friends when you let them know you are getting divorced. Some friends will drift away from you, some may become staunch allies of your former mate, some may make you feel so bad each time you talk to them that you talk to them less and less often.

On the other hand, some friends will become your mainstays, volunteering to pick you up at the airport late Monday night, inviting you to dinner or the movies on a regular basis, including you and your children in holiday plans. These friends are worth their weight in gold. Let the others go and nurture these relationships by returning the favor when you can, and by expressing your gratitude.

New friends are likely to turn up too—people you know more casually, who are moved by their feeling for you, or by memories of what divorce was like for them, to come forward and offer a friendly ear or some good, solid advice based on their own experience. These relationships may be only temporary, but they do not have to last a lifetime to be valuable.

- Nurture the friendship of good friends, by saying thanks and reciprocating their favors.
- Let withering friendships go with as little regret or analysis as possible.
- Open the door to new friendships, even if they seem to be based only on your current situation.

Laurin, divorced after eleven years, no children, says, "When I told my best friend, Grace, that Ted and I were separating, I was surprised that she was so cool about it. She said she was sorry to hear the news, and offered to help me in any way she could, but there was a sort of warmth missing when she was talking to me. I tried to ignore it. I'd call her up like usual to pour my heart out to her. But I wasn't getting what I needed. She'd try to argue me out of my feelings, or she'd say, 'Well, if you look at this from Ted's point of view . . . ' That was the last thing I wanted to do right then! I don't know exactly what bothered her so much about our divorce, but she was definitely bothered by it. After the first couple of months, I started getting together with some women I met in a group for newly separated people. They were ideal companions. Our experiences were different, but our problems and feelings were similar enough that we could really help each other. And I guess being on equal ground was a big factor in our relationship, too. Grace and I aren't as close as we used to be, but we are friends. Our lives are pretty different now, too, so I guess what happened between us is just part of the normal course of things. Things change all the time. It keeps it interesting!"

36.

Count your blessings.

❧ ❧ ❧

There is always something left to love. And if you ain't learned that, you ain't learned nothing.
—LORRAINE HANSBERRY

Your efforts to stay on top of all the changes in your life right now may lead you to be quite self-absorbed for the moment. It's natural to be feeling sorry for yourself.

If the complications of separation and divorce are getting you down, you may feel cut off from everyone just because your own moods are a barrier, preventing you from seeing everything that is available to you from friends, family, and even some acquaintances. You may not be making use of all the things that are going well for you, all the things you can count on for yourself.

Look around. You may be glossing over some real treasures among your friends and relatives, people who have been signalling that you are important to them, that they care about you, even if your contact with them is not deep or frequent.

Take time to appreciate the phone call from a high school friend who, having just heard about your divorce, calls to say she's been there herself and she knows you'll come through okay. You don't have to schedule a visit with her unless you want to. Just let yourself feel that hand on your shoulder.

Do you have a good job? Great! Pay attention to the way your colleagues may have tried to lighten your workdays recently. Thank them.

Do you live in a neighborhood you like? Well, at least that's settled.

You can do a lot to nourish yourself and to lift yourself out of that feeling of being alone in the world by doing a thorough accounting of all the gestures of love and good will, all the daily triumphs, large and small, that are yours. Maybe they are not enough. Maybe they are not what you want. But don't discount them.

Keep a list of everything that is good in your life. When someone does something nice, when you experience a feeling of success or happiness, add it to your list. Then when you find yourself stuck in the rut of feeling that everything in your life has gone wrong, read it over. Take a look at how much has gone right.

> ∾ Don't make more of what's gone wrong in your life than you make of what has gone well.

> ∾ Take time to write a list of all the good things that are yours so you can read it over whenever you need to.

> ∾ Make a habit of counting your blessings whenever you feel self-pity creeping up on you.

Brenda is forty-eight. "Both my husband and I had been married before," she says. "We have one son together and I have two stepsons, his children. They are both over twenty-one and live out of town. Very frequently, and I've heard other people say this, stepchildren and stepparents are lost to each other when a marriage breaks up, because the children are not sure why the marriage ended, whether you did it to their parent, what really happened. I'm having a very interesting experience that was brought home to me on Mother's Day. Both my stepsons were in touch with me on Mother's Day. The older one sent me an absolutely beautiful, loving letter, and the younger one called, as if I were their mother, saying in effect that I am as much their mother in some ways as their true mother is. I was so moved by that because my enormous terror was that my son would lose his brothers, that I would lose this extended family that I had helped to create, and that we'd all end up being hostile and angry. In fact, it hasn't been that way. I've got some major financial difficulties at the moment, and their father and I are not on good terms. But it's nice to be able to give myself some credit for whatever it is I've been able to communicate to those young men. I'm very grateful to realize we won't be lost to each other."

37.

Be realistic and creative about finances.

❧ ❧ ❧

Money is always dull, except when you haven't got any, and then it's terrifying.

—SHEILA BISHOP

Every money problem has a solution. Some demand more creativity than others.

If you have not before been accustomed to managing the entire scope of personal finance, prepare to get used to it.

You can begin by talking to someone you trust who knows about money. That may be someone in your family, a close friend or a professional financial advisor or accountant. Take some time to study your financial situation and to carefully calculate your needs and capabilities. Make sure you consider retirement needs, health insurance needs, expenses for education, and other long-range issues. You may not have to alter your lifestyle very much, or you may have to make some radical changes. Whatever your needs are, you *will* be able to meet them if you plan realistically.

If you feel as if you are fast on your way to the poorhouse, take a look at the divorced women around you. Are any of them in debtor's prison? Sudden financial changes can be scary, but you can adjust and survive.

The most serious mistakes to watch out for are refusing to face facts, or refusing to take full responsibility for your finances. If you have less money than you had when you were married, and most women do have less, you will have to decide how to cut down on spending, and then you will have to actually cut down.

You can, of course, tackle this problem from the other direction by deciding how you can earn more money. Look for ways that will not place an undue burden on you. Don't pile on too much moonlighting when you are stressed, unless you absolutely have to. Do you have room for a roommate or a boarder? Can you cut childcare expenses and add to your income simultaneously by offering reduced rent in exchange for part-time babysitting? Do you have a garage you can rent out?

Look for long-term solutions to financial challenges. A yard sale is a lot of work and you can earn money from it only once. Turning one of your interests into a part-time business, however, is an investment of your time that may grow to give you more financial stability. Use your imagination.

- Don't panic about finances, just attend to them realistically.
- Separate short-term needs from long-range plans. Don't let short-term problems push you toward unhelpful, temporary solutions.
- Keep track of your priorities and make plans to meet them.

"When I got divorced," says Stephanie, 41, "my problems followed me out of town to the state where I'd been offered a new and wonderful job. I was in a lot of debt when I got there, but my salary was so much better and the cost of living was so much lower that I thought everything would solve itself. In my excitement, I got a whole new wardrobe and rented a big, beautiful house for my son and me. The next thing I knew, I had huge credit card balances that I was having trouble paying, and when I got into an accident with my car, it put me in a pretty precarious financial position. After I stopped panicking, I tried to calmly assess my situation. I made a budget for myself that included paying a certain amount on the credit cards the minute the bills came in so that I wouldn't be tempted to spend it elsewhere. I put the credit

cards in my safe deposit box so that I wouldn't be tempted to use them. Then, because I live in a college town, I realized that I could rent out a room and bath in the house without any trouble. That helped us out a lot, and even gave me the comfort of having another adult in the house, and someone to watch the place when I had to go out of town. It took a year, but I'm out of debt now and I learned some things about how to manage. Now I can think about things like funding my retirement plan, saving for Kit's college. All that usual stuff. Those sleepless nights are gone."

38.

Rescue yourself instead of waiting to be rescued.

❧ ❧ ❧

Heroes take journeys, confront dragons, and discover the treasure of their true selves.
—CAROL PEARSON

Stories of heroes usually begin with self-doubt. By the end of the story, the hero learns through experience to replace doubt with self-confidence.

You have everything you need to proceed with your life. No one else can provide anything that you do not already have. All you need to do is to learn to gain access to all the power that is already within you.

The more you forge ahead with your life, the more you demonstrate to yourself that you are a powerful person. If you wait for someone else to rescue you, if you persist in telling yourself that you are not up to taking care of yourself alone, you will be cheating yourself of getting to know your best self. Worse, you will add to your sense of worthlessness, rather than rescuing yourself from it.

You know how to solve problems. You know how to carry responsibilities. You know how to live with risk, how to cope with disasters, how to get up in the morning and get going. Look at how much you have accomplished in your life.

If you want someone to love you and take care of you, you can have that. It will happen sooner and work out better if you learn how to love yourself and take care of yourself before that other person is in view. If you cast someone else as the hero rather than working things out for yourself, you will never have an equal relationship, never feel the joy of being truly independent, never be rid of fear.

It is much more fun to be the hero than it is to be the damsel in distress. It's a role you can play happily, and for the rest of your life.

- Once you learn how to take care of yourself emotionally, you will carry that ability with you always.

- Learning to be self-reliant is the best preparation for beginning healthy relationships with other people.

- You can do more for yourself, more lastingly, than anyone else can.

"I'm another person," says Jean, 54, who divorced fifteen years ago when her four children were all still at home. "Nobody would even recognize me. I grew up. By the time I got a divorce I understood what people mean when they say that love is not enough. My husband loved me, but he also couldn't stop himself from hurting me—I mean physically. I also understood that I was responsible for myself. I didn't understand that for most of my marriage. I knew how to be materially responsible—I'm the oldest of seven children, so I was always very responsible and I understood that. But emotionally to take care of myself, I didn't know that I could be responsible for my own emotional health. I learned that, and that I really could take care of myself, and that's a good thing to know. I took classes and went to seminars. I went into therapy. I did a lot of things to learn about myself, to learn how to take care of myself so that I wouldn't fall into the trap of looking for somebody who would agree to take care of me. I learned what I set

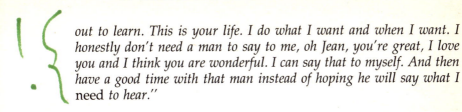

out to learn. This is your life. I do what I want and when I want. I honestly don't need a man to say to me, oh Jean, you're great, I love you and I think you are wonderful. I can say that to myself. And then have a good time with that man instead of hoping he will say what I need to hear."

39.

Discover the joys of being capable and independent.

꙳ ꙳ ꙳

If you want good service, serve yourself.
—SPANISH PROVERB

It isn't hard to be independent. It's much harder not to be. Once you've decided you don't want to be rescued after all and begin to explore your own capabilities and talents, you may not want to give them up again.

When you've gained enough knowledge of the way your car works to talk to your mechanic as if you know what you're talking about, why would you ever want to go back to not-so-blissful ignorance?

When you've taken charge of your own finances and discovered you have a talent for choosing investments wisely, why would you ever want to stop choosing for yourself?

It feels good to know your way around a hardware store, to drive off for a vacation by yourself, to know where all the circuit breakers are.

For good reasons, marriage encourages people to depend upon each other. When the marriage is working well, that's fine. Even feminists are allowed to share responsibilities. When you find yourself with no one to share those chores with, you can feel very let down and overburdened. The best way to beat that feeling is to realize that you are faced with an opportunity to add to your skills.

It may turn out that you understand your computer better than your former husband did, that the family checkbook always balances at the end of the month now that you're in charge, that you like to prune the bushes. And if you don't like some of these tasks, hire some help with them. Barter an exchange of chores with a friend: I'll help you with your taxes if you help me caulk the bathtub. Expand your talents.

- Think of the new range of tasks you are faced with as adult education opportunities. The tuition is free.
- Practice your new skills and use your new knowledge with pride.
- You don't have to do *everything* yourself, but you should enjoy what you do for yourself.

"There was a gradual transition when my husband and I separated," says Sharon, 39. *"I was in the same house, with the kitchen cabinets he had built. It felt like 'our house.' I had the hardest time learning to say 'my car' instead of 'our car' or 'the car.' Just about the time I learned to say 'my car' I totalled it, so that was that! But then I bought my own house. Just doing that was very exhilarating. And once I moved in I realized what a difference it made to be in a place that was mine alone. To be doing this all myself was very different. I had never done anything like that before. I'd now gotten a mortgage by myself! We'd never owned a house before, so Sam had never even done that. And I painted the whole house with a friend. Then I was becoming knowledgeable about all kinds of quaint plumbing and stuff, and I was getting strong muscles from moving things around myself, and a good sense of 'I can do it.' I bought a brand-new car by myself. It was an ordeal. I got so much advice I didn't know what to do with*

it all. But, hey, I'd already bought a house, right? I love my house. I even love mowing the yard. My husband complained about doing it more than he did it. I have a tiny yard, so it's just enough work for me. I'm really proud of myself. I did this!"

40.

Remember: A divorce takes years, not days to get through.

ॐ ॐ ॐ

One does not die from pain unless one chooses to.
—WAKAKO YAMAUCHI

Divorce occurs so frequently among men and women today that people are inclined to speak of it in terms that don't do justice to what a lengthy and complicated process it usually is. We say, "They got a divorce," as if getting the decree is a simple legal matter.

Even the legal aspects of divorce take more time to settle than most people realize, usually about two years. Depending upon your own psychology and what entanglements you meet up with along the way, the psychological process of divorce may take many more years than that. For some people, alas, it is never complete.

Rushing through the legal requirements of divorce will not necessarily help you get over the pain of divorce any more quickly. In fact, a rush to settlement can cause more problems in the future than it solves in the present.

There is nothing you can do to hurry yourself out of your hurt. What you can do, however, is use this painful time to recognize that, like any mourning we do, divorce has stages, and you can work at healing your wounds with consciousness and care, so that you may set yourself on a positive course for the future.

You can't help feeling sorry for yourself at times, but stopping there will leave you nowhere. Use those introspective moments to take an inventory of the strengths and weaknesses that were a part of your marriage. Look toward what you can do in the future to carry the strengths with you, to replace the weaknesses with new strengths.

You will also simply need to be patient while time does its work. Things *do* change—even when you don't want them to. If you want to feel better, you will. In time.

- Be extra good to yourself, and patient with yourself, while time does its work to heal the wounds of divorce.

- Understand that there is little you can do to hurry this process.

- Allow yourself to mourn your marriage so that you can then put grief behind you.

Eleanor, 58, says, "I was married for thirty-three years. I have four children from twenty-nine to thirty-five, and one granddaughter. I didn't want out of the marriage. My husband did. And now I can see some of the ways in which our marriage had not been working well for quite some time. Anyway, he fell madly in love with a woman who was almost his daughter's age and in a way that made it much easier for me because I could say I'm not thirty-four years old anymore. I'm many years older than that, so there is nothing I can do if that's what he wants. It was devastating at the time and I thought that I could never live it through. But it's amazing, as time goes by—I've been divorced about three years and separated about five—how much things have changed. I can remember people telling me I had to give it time and I would say I don't want to hear that, I am miserable and I can't live through this. But now I think that's about the best advice I remember hearing: Give it time, give it time. Try to be easy on yourself, and good to yourself, and let time do its work. The other thing people would say is just think of all the growth you're going to do through this trial and tribulation, which was something else I didn't want to hear. But then as I look back on it, I did grow a lot. I like myself much, much better now. There is an awful lot to what they said that is true."

41.

Look to the future as if you can make it happen. You can.

☙ ☙ ☙

I can only say what I myself have learned: that life's purpose is to grow.

—LE LY HAYSLIP

You cannot rewrite the past. But the future—ah, the future! It is all yours.

It's important to keep your eyes front, looking to what lies ahead of you. In many ways, the future offers you more possibilities now than it did when you were married. Even the best marriages impose limits on us, just by the fact of our having to consider another person's needs and desires along with our own.

You're on your own again now. And that gives you some freedom to dream. What is it that you really want from life? Where and how would you be living if you could live anywhere you wanted? Those are the questions you should base your plans on. There is no good reason to feel stuck with the blueprint of your old life. There is no reason to be guided by "I can't," or "But I always used to..." You are not less than you were. You are more. This is your new life. You can make it as new as you want.

Make a wish list for yourself of all the things you want your life to include. Be imaginative. Don't censor ideas because they seem impossible to accomplish. When you are satisfied that your list is a good one, that you have really dreamed big, start thinking about what it would actually take for you to bring some of the most important things on your list into being. Have you always wanted to live on the other side of the country? Okay, what would you have to do to get yourself there? Have you dreamed of sailing in the Virgin Islands? How can you make that happen? Want to study t'ai chi? Why not? Call the chamber of commerce in a city you're attracted to, call a sailing school, call a t'ai chi center for information. Today. That will be Step One.

If you take your dreams and heart's desires seriously, you can plan to make them happen in just the same way that you plan for three meals a day. Those three meals end up on the table like clockwork because you think of them as necessary. Why not think of some of your dreams as necessary too? Life is for the living. It's up to you to make sure you are alive.

- ☙ Think of your dreams as real possibilities.
- ☙ Plan realistic steps to make your dreams come true.
- ☙ Don't hesitate: take some of those steps *now*. Then keep stepping.

Felicia, 36, was married for ten years and had a four-year-old son when she and her husband separated. "One of my best friends has lived in Oregon for many years. I visited her as often as I could and I was always drawn to the life she had there. I love the landscape, the weather, the openness of the people. I'd always thought it would be wonderful to live there but I didn't let myself get too far into it because Jim is a physician and he had a successful practice in New Jersey. It wasn't realistic to think about picking up and moving across the country. When we first split up, I thought I had to stay where I was for Gavin's sake, so he could be near his father. But I wasn't happy. I had a lot of years ahead of me. I kept imagining how beautiful life could be, for both of us, out West. It was a powerful wish. I began calling some of the school districts in the areas I liked, just to check on job possibilities in special ed, which is my field. I spoke to Jim about my thoughts. At first he was very uptight, very much against it. He felt that I would be taking Gavin away from him. But we have had pretty good cooperation in our parenting since we split, so we were able to imagine an arrangement that could work. Then I put on a lot of steam in my job search, and I found a position that was good enough for me to take that leap and move out here. I have never been so happy. We've been out here two years now and it's everything I kept thinking it would be. I love my job, Gavin is getting to be a real outdoors kind of kid, it's perfect. His dad flies him back home every time there's a long enough break from school, and Gavin spends most of the summer back there. So far so good.''

42.

Avoid the bitter aftertaste
of bitterness.

જી જી જી

*Vinegar he poured on me all his life; I am well marinated;
how can I be honey now?*

—TILLIE OLSEN

Maybe you know a woman whose life seemed to come to an
end when her marriage ended. Lodged in resentment, she keeps
herself on a narrow road between what was and what is no more.
She does not have to do that. And you don't.

The one thing you always have control over is your attitude.
That's a powerful thing. You will have to work to understand how
to get and keep control of your attitude, what tricks work on you
in particular to help jostle you out of a bad mood, out of getting
lost in the swamp of regret and blame. You can do it.

In the long run, it doesn't matter who was right or wrong.
What's done is done. Get over it. If you choose to keep attending
to all the wrongs that have been done to you, you will make them
enormously important, give them much more power over you than
they should have. You will live in the bleak atmosphere of the
victim until you choose not to stay there any longer.

Once you choose to let go and look ahead, you will really be
taking control of your life. You cannot change what happened. You
cannot change other people. You can only keep working to change
your outlook, to keep it as positive as possible.

If you find yourself having the same negative thoughts over and over again, and if it seems that you never make any progress with them but simply repeat the pattern of making yourself miserable day after day, get some help. See a counselor or seek out a support group where you can talk about these feelings and get some solid advice to help you get past them.

There is a big difference between the kind of introspection that leads to insight and problem-solving and the kind that only dredges up bad feelings and bad memories without resolving them. Be honest with yourself about where you are allowing your thoughts to wander.

- Be careful in allowing bitterness into your heart. It may take over.
- You have to live with yourself. Work on making yourself pleasant to live with.
- Be aware of the difference between problem-solving and dwelling on problems. One is helpful, the other is not.

Edith, 53, says, "My ex-husband left me for another woman, one of his colleagues. I have never seen her since they are married, although I did know who she was, and knew that they had had an affair. Sometimes in vengeance I think, well, okay. I had him for the best years and now she'll have to take care of him in his decline. But I don't have any dealings with her. I don't know what it would be like when the day comes that one of my children gets married and invites Dad and his wife. I probably have just built a monster about that. Hopefully, if I do have to see her I will find that it's easier than I imagined it would be. Time takes care of a lot, that I know. At first, I wanted my husband to die. He knew it, too. He felt very guilty. I got over my bitterness by focusing on my side of things. When he left I felt he was all wrong. He was the bastard who did a deed like that. We'd been married twenty-eight years; we'd had some ups and downs but we both admit we'd had some wonderful times. So, little by little I began to look back and see my side of the equation. And there is a big side of what I contributed to the marriage and why he then became unhappy. I'm still working on these issues in therapy. We never communicated. We never really said how we felt when one or the other of us did something we didn't like. We both kept it inside thinking it would go away. I think we both played a part. When I did some of that analysis, and when my life had settled into new routines that I am comfortable with and enjoy, I felt less concerned with what he had done. I'm more interested in what I'm doing now, and what I'm going to do next."

43.

Make some demands
on your new life.

ॐ ॐ ॐ

The revolution begins at home.
—CHERRÍE MORAGA AND GLORIA ANZALDÙA

You don't have to settle for much that you don't want to settle
for. You don't have to stay forever in a job you don't like, you
don't have to spend time with people you don't enjoy, you don't
have to carry more than your share of the load. You don't even
have to live with an ugly living room couch.

The life you have now is probably much more flexible than you
think. Do you wish you could make some new friends? Then don't
sit home thinking, "Now is not the best time. I have too many
problems and too much work to do." Go out and socialize. Make
time in your life for that if it is important to you. Then the problems will begin to solve themselves more easily; the work will
seem lighter.

If you want your life to be good to you, you must build the life
you want. The more you go out to meet life head-on, instead of
hanging back, afraid of the next blow life may deliver, the better
you will feel. About everything.

Insist on the best for yourself. Eat what you like, spend time
with friends that you like, read books that you like, go to movies
that you like. Replace that ugly living room couch, or cover it with
some fabulous fabric. You can be good to yourself without spend-

126

ing a lot of money. Whatever it takes, don't settle for a poor fit. If you continue to wear ill-fitting shoes just because they are almost new and cost a lot, the only thing you will get for your pains is sore feet.

Keep your suffering to a minimum by demanding a good life for yourself. Demand that life give back to you what you are willing to give to your life. If you want a better job, direct some concentrated effort toward finding one—rather than wishing for one—and you will get there. This is a truth you can demonstrate to yourself. Every phone call not made is nothing but a phone call not made. Every call you make is one more opportunity to turn your life in the direction you want it to go. Honor yourself by demanding a good life for yourself and taking action to meet it.

- Don't ask too little of yourself or of your new life.
- There is no need to let anyone but yourself dictate the terms of your future.
- It's true: Where there's a will, there's a way.

"I don't even like to think about how drastically the terms of my life changed when I was getting divorced," says Nancy, 46. "I'd never worried about money, never compromised on where I wanted to live or what I wanted to wear, or what kind of vacation we took. Suddenly, my options were very different. I went through anger, fear, depression—all the typical phases of feeling the loss of my life. People kept telling me I had to compromise now, I had to be realistic, I had to live very carefully and not expect that the same things were available to me. That made me more furious! More depressed! But I did have one friend, a man, who kept telling me I could have anything I wanted if I decided I wanted it badly enough. At first I didn't even understand what he was saying. How can you drink champagne on a beer budget? It took quite a while for me to see that you can—just not every day. Then I began to figure out how to have the things I wanted. And of course they have turned out to be different from what I had, but nicer and more suited to me in many ways because I chose them thought-

fully, I wasn't following the program for 'the good life' anymore. I moved to a neighborhood I'd never considered before, and I love it. People are friendlier; there are nicer trees. My house is not grand, but I've fixed it up exactly the way I want it to be. The colors are my colors. The bonus is that I've found out a lot more about what I actually like and don't like. And, honestly, I'm proud of doing it for myself."

44.

Accept the truth: There is no such thing as security.

🐿 🐿 🐿

Only in growth, reform, and change, paradoxically enough, is true security to be found.
—ANNE MORROW LINDBERGH

One of our basic drives as human beings leads us to seek safety and security for ourselves, and to be cautious about taking risks. Your marriage may have given you a sense of security at one time. Now that it is over, how can you feel safe and grounded again?

Having your source of security suddenly taken away is shocking and frightening. Some people react by making panicky attempts to hold on to it, or by trying to replace it immediately. But the truth is, there is no such thing as security. Just living on planet Earth is proof enough of that, when entire nations can disappear overnight!

A sense of security is only a feeling. It is *not* security. Rather than trying to hold tight to symbols of safety, you can achieve far more *real* security by learning to be flexible and not so dependent on keeping things the same. If you become interested in change, really interested instead of being afraid of it, you will be much better equipped to deal with whatever happens next than you will be if the only solution that you can think of is to build everything out of bricks.

Think about the story of the Three Little Pigs. One pig foolishly built a house of straw that the Big Bad Wolf blew down in one breath. The next pig built his of sticks, but it, too, was easily destroyed. The really smart pig built his house of bricks. Safe and secure, right? Well, maybe the wolf couldn't blow down the house of bricks, but he got in anyway. What saved the pigs was their inventiveness: they had a kettle of boiling water waiting for him when he dropped down the chimney.

Feeling insecure can actually give you positive motivation to take some risks, and to put yourself out there in ways that you may not have done before. The need to make more money may lead you to a better job or a fulfilling business venture. The need to fortify yourself with stronger social relationships may lead you to meet wonderful new friends. You may discover skills and talents you didn't know you had until you were put to the test.

What do you really need to feel safe? Sometimes the more you have, the more you worry about what would happen if you lost it. Some people may have more material success. It is true that money can improve the quality of life, but people with more money than you have do not necessarily have more security. If you take stock of your own abilities to get along with what you do have, and if you continue to be interested in the future, you should find that you have what you need.

- ❧ Security is an illusion.
- ❧ Your talents, skills, and, above all, your flexibility and belief in yourself are priceless assets.
- ❧ Working without a net can make you perform at the top of your ability.

Computer consultant Justine, thirty-six and married eleven years, says, "If my former husband had come to me and said, look, the house is yours and you'll have this much . . . I'd have said, 'Bye! I think a lot of the anguish in getting divorced had to do with feeling so vulnerable financially, and feeling so insecure. And I was actually making enough money for my daughter and me to live on. But I work for myself and it's so uncertain. What if I'm in a car wreck tomorrow and I can't do my work? It's a little scary. I've coped with it all by, first of all, looking back and saying, 'Okay, so far nothing really bad has ever happened.' And it really hasn't. Second of all, I try to reassure myself by getting the best health insurance I can, the best disability insurance I can. I try to save so that if I don't get any work in six months I can survive. Then, I get out there and try to sell myself, try to bring in more business. You know what they say about the hungry salesperson—she's the one who makes the sale. When I stop and look around I can see that nobody has a sure thing. That woman down the block whose husband was told he had to give her sixty thousand dollars a year because she's a 'displaced homemaker,' has no more security than I do. What if her former husband dies, or loses his job, or doesn't send checks anymore? Worse yet, she has no experience with the job market. What does she have to fall back on? Everybody has those worries. Not just you. Not just me. So if you can choose to be an optimist about it, why would you choose to be a pessimist?"

45.

Tie up loose ends,
the sooner the better.

༒ ༒ ༒

I want now to be of today. It is painful to be conscious of two worlds.

—MARY ANTIN

Even after all the legal questions of divorce have been settled, most people are left with details to resolve. It may be that you have furniture or photographs left to divide between your two households, or some other property that you own in common. It may be that you have had difficulty deciding on a firm schedule for time spent with your children, or on where the children will spend which holidays. Sometimes even larger issues remain unresolved because dealing with them has been simply too difficult.

Whatever the difficulties, it's better for everyone to bring as much as possible to a conclusion at the time of divorce. If it is painful to look through the family photographs and decide who gets what, it will continue to be painful every time you look at them, or even glance at the box you are afraid to open. What appears to allow you to avoid pain may actually be causing you to experience that pain in small doses over and over again.

As you and your former mate move further into your new lives, your priorities for resolving what has been left unfinished are likely to move further and further apart. Rather than have those issues become sore points between you, try to get as much as possible tied up quickly, while what you had in common is still clear.

Loose ends are not really untied. They are tied to the past. Sometimes people leave loose ends because they have not completely accepted the idea that what is gone is gone. You might find, however, that once these things are resolved, a better basis exists for holding on to the good memories and being able to look at them without feeling so torn, and that a much better basis exists for beginning a new kind of positive relationship with your former mate.

- Be conscious of what you are leaving undone. How soon can it be resolved?
- Loose ends may delay the healing process for everyone involved in your divorce.
- You will have a better basis for a workable relationship with your former mate if as much as possible has been resolved between you.

"My ex-husband, we had a little beach cottage together," says Mary Alice, 49. "And he wanted us to still keep it, and to just take turns using it. It's incredibly romantic, you know, with the sound of the ocean outside all night. I could never sleep there again if I thought he'd slept there with somebody else. I could never take my new husband there. I mean, that one was easy. It was like, 'Forget it.' But some other areas are murkier. We had been saving for our daughter's education together, making decisions together about how to invest the money. Finally, I realized we should just save separately, deal with it separately, even though we shared the cost when she went to college. And there were certain occasions we were used to spending with friends. At first we would talk about what to do every time one of them came up— who should go, who should not go. These were always painful discussions. So it got better when we just fell into new habits about who went where and it was no longer under discussion anymore, because for a long time we really couldn't share those occasions,

couldn't both be there. I find that peace of mind among my divorced friends comes with clearer lines of separation and definitiveness about life. Part of it is putting it away, putting it behind. In a lot of ways, you just can't merge your former life with the life you are living now. When you have truly launched your new life, you won't even want to merge the old one with it as much."

46.

Look before you leap into new commitments.

🐎 🐎 🐎

The Real is the sole foundation of the Ideal.
—Grace Aguilar

Pairing up is natural for all mature living things. People want to love and be loved, to have someone with whom they can share the experiences of their days and nights.

It is not only that loving feeling that is lost when people get divorced, but the structure of a paired life as well. In some ways, you may miss that structure more than you miss the person who helped provide it, more than you miss being in love.

Being single again may make you feel exposed, vulnerable, uncertain of yourself or of how to be out in the world alone. Some women retreat from the world for a time, choosing to put their social lives on hold. Others rush out to meet someone new to conquer that "something is missing" feeling.

If you are eager to be paired up again, you will be wise to give yourself some time to explore your options. You probably wouldn't buy the first house you look at when you are deciding where to live, so why should you settle for the first available partner?

Transitions can be frightening because everything is so up in the air. It can be frightening to be alone, too. It's a good idea to look

into those fears, rather than to wish them away by clinging to
someone new.

During this time of transition, you are learning a lot about yourself. This knowledge is essential to establishing a strong foundation
for your life from now on. Take time to allow yourself to become
well-acquainted with your own likes and dislikes, your own
wishes and plans for the future, before you try to make them fit
with anyone else's.

If you really don't like being alone, don't be. It's fine to have a
companion, or a series of companions beginning whenever you feel
ready. Just hold off on making promises too soon or too hastily.
You may even begin to relax and enjoy playing the field for a
while.

- &. Learn what you want from new relationships before making
  any commitments.
- &. Why compromise? You *can* have what you want.
- &. When you are more at ease with your own life you will have
  a better chance of finding and building a good, new long-
  term relationship.

*"I've learned that I can live by myself quite comfortably," says
Liz, 52. "When I first came back to Virginia after my husband
asked for a divorce, I met someone right away through a single
parents organization and went out with him for about a year. And
I kept saying to myself, 'Wouldn't it be lovely if I could just fall in
love with him because that would solve my problem: I wouldn't
have to be single.' And after about a year or a year and a half I
realized there was just no way. I couldn't do it for that reason. I'd
rather live by myself than with someone who wasn't quite right. If
we'd gotten married, it would have lasted a very short time. I'm
getting more particular as time goes by. My time is valuable to me.
When I was in college, if a man called me and I thought he was
even mildly interesting, I'd go out with him. Now I'd rather spend*

the time with friends or at home with a book, rather than go out with someone just because he is male. I can do a lot on my own. I've even learned to go to the movies alone— and like it! And I don't lack for men friends, either, thank you very much!"

47.

Remember the good parts.

❧ ❧ ❧

Memories stretch and pull around me—Bark drying on a new canoe.

—MARY TALLMOUNTAIN

Life is a process of becoming. None of us is a finished product, not at any step along the way. We can't completely discard any of those steps without losing important parts of ourselves.

Going through a painful divorce may make you yearn to wish away your past, to erase all the painful memories that keep popping up to torment you. Wouldn't it be easier to start with a clean slate?

No one has to remain trapped in the past. Still, if you do not come to terms with the past, sifting out what is worth keeping from it, you will suffer a much greater loss than you need to.

Your marriage was a big part of your life. More than likely, it began with hope and promise for the future and held a lot of happy moments. Those are yours to keep, regardless of what followed. It's up to you to nurture the good memories, when you are ready to start doing that, and not to let them be overwhelmed by memories that stir feelings of hurt and sadness.

Sometimes people seem to think that we learn and grow only by examining our mistakes and our traumas. But you can put the past to work for you by emphasizing the memories that give you knowledge and support for moving on with your life, and de-emphasizing those that bring you to a halt by filling you with regret.

Your personal history belongs to you more surely than does anything else in your life. It is filled with things that can show you how far you have come, how much you have accomplished, what a good time you have been having, if you look for those things. And you should look for them, rather than turn your back on the whole story because some parts of it are unhappy.

- Keep the good parts. They are yours.
- There is as much to learn from what went right as from what went wrong.
- Looking at the good in your life helps create more of it.

Rosanne, 57, says, "I was married for such a long time and in many ways I appreciate the years we were married. I don't want to think of it as twenty-seven years lost. My kids have a hard time with their father. The divorce knocked him off his pedestal. I helped my daughter open the door to a better relationship with him when she came to me and said she didn't know how to feel close to him anymore. I told her to send him a tape of some of the music she likes lately, because he would be able to relate to that, and comment on it. She likes jazz and so does he. At first I wondered why I had bothered to involve myself at all, but then I thought, why shouldn't I? Because he in many ways is a nice human being, and I want to remember that. You shouldn't have to throw away everything; you should be able to keep the good parts. I feel, in a way, that during our marriage I lived in his world. As I look back on it, there were many things I gained and learned from being in his world. I was brought up with opera and classical music, and he was brought up with jazz and folk music, which to me was a totally unknown quantity. I look back on it and I think how much I gained through what he brought to my life. Why should I let go of that? Those are the things that validate my long marriage. I want to keep the good parts."

48.

Assess the new you and take her strengths into the future.

❧ ❧ ❧

I change myself, I change the world.
—GLORIA ANZALDÚA

What have you learned from your own divorce? Probably a lot. And more to come.

As you pull yourself through this trial by fire, you will find that you are a changed woman. You know more about life now than you did before, more about yourself, more about your strengths and weaknesses, your likes and dislikes. Even if you were not trying to learn any of these things, you ought to be glad that there is at least some compensation for your trouble.

Pay attention to the new tools that are turning up in your toolbox. How are you wiser? More demanding of yourself and of what life has to offer? What pitfalls have you learned to avoid by learning how to recognize them?

Maybe you thought you couldn't live alone. Now you know you can. Maybe you were afraid of handling finances for yourself, of dealing with car salesmen, or of looking for a better job. Now you have done some of those things, and you know you can do them.

Experience is a terrific teacher. Anyone who has been through a divorce feels not only older but wiser. That wisdom doesn't have to make you shy away from taking risks. It should instead make you feel better equipped to succeed, and to be willing to take risks you might not have taken before.

Your self-confidence may have suffered through divorce, yet it may even at the same time have grown in some ways. And it should continue to grow as you continue to demonstrate to yourself that you are strong, stronger than ever, and capable of using what you have learned to shape a new life that suits you.

- ⤫ Congratulate yourself for everything you have learned.
- ⤫ Think about how that new knowledge can work for you from now on.
- ⤫ Keep high standards for what you expect from yourself.

"After fifteen years of my marriage I felt as low as you can imagine," says Sharon, 46. "Getting out of that marriage taught me something about self-respect. I've learned to take care of myself by not letting things slide. I used to be the kind of person who if my husband said something really hurtful to me, it always didn't matter. I thought if I made any protest, he would go away and not like me anymore. I thought that about everyone. Really, I wasn't giving anyone enough credit by thinking that their feelings for me were so shallow. In the past, I'd say I'm such a horrible person, I'm going to change myself, I'll turn myself inside out to do what he wants. That's a big example of the way that I have changed. This is it. This is me. Take me as I am. My new marriage is completely different. For a long time I didn't drive. I have had cerebral palsy since birth on one side and in my family, when it came to physical dexterity, there was always the assumption that I couldn't do it. The whole time I was with my ex-husband I didn't drive. I was afraid to. Mel, my current husband, didn't like my being so dependent in that way. He insisted that I learn to drive when I first started seeing him. He was already very important to me, but even though I'd already been thinking about learning to drive I told him, 'I will never drive. Never ever. Don't like it? I'll see

ya.' And he really had to think about it until finally he said, 'Okay. I want you. Never drive. That's fine.' That's when I started taking driving lessons, when he said to me, 'I take you as you are.' I don't settle for less than that anymore."

49.

Resolve your power struggle with your former mate.

❧ ❧ ❧

Power . . . is not an end in itself, but is an instrument that must be used toward an end.

—JEANE J. KIRKPATRICK

As long as you continue to struggle with your former mate over who's in charge, you will not be in possession of your own full power.

Once the major issues of your divorce have been hammered out, try to put down your hammer as soon as you can. It's unlikely that everything between you will go the way you have wanted it to, but continuing to make issues out of it will only prolong the most painful phases of divorce and keep you living in the past longer than is necessary.

By focusing on your own life, the one that is separate from his, you can keep sight of your own personal goals, your own accomplishments. As these grow, the differences between you and your former mate will become less and less important. You do not have to win every point to come out a winner.

If he brings your son home a half hour late from a dinner date, is that worth fighting about? You'll know you are making progress with your own emotions when you can say calmly, "Please call if you're running late again," rather than "If you bring him home this late again I won't let him go out with you on school nights."

There may be some real issues between you that do call for you to stand up for yourself or your children. Be clear about sorting those out from issues that arise purely from emotional reactions to being divorced and having to deal with someone you probably need a break from dealing with. Stand up when it matters. Back off when it really isn't a big deal. When you care more consistently about keeping peace than you do about being right and being vindicated, you'll benefit by living a more peaceful existence. Everyone around you will benefit by that too.

- Sort out significant issues from those you can afford to let go.
- Make peace for yourself by not looking for things to be angry about.
- Keep your focus on the accomplishments in your new life and build on those.

"The first year he tried to take one of the children and not the other to his house for the summer," says Marina, 38, *"because one of them was mad at him and said she didn't want to see him. That I could not allow, because it would have hurt both the kids. I said he had to have both of them come, so he did, but for a shorter time. We were in a terrible power struggle the whole first year. The kids were dealing with a new stepmother within seven weeks of the divorce, and I had moved with them to a new city. Now I don't feel threatened by him anymore. They're doing really well here, I'm doing really well here. Good job for me, good school for them. I used to say to their father, it was such a thing with me: 'You're not going to get one more day with them than that divorce settlement says you have.' Now I give in. I let him have the kids for the whole summer instead of half. They're sixteen and fourteen. They need to have a relationship with their father. What I was saying before was out of hurt and anger. As they became more grounded and adjusted to our new life, I was less worried about losing them.*

They were mad at their father but they took it out on me, so I wanted to take it out on him. I'd like to say we worked it out, but what really worked it out was time. Everyone has to stop jockeying for position as you do in the beginning. You just have to get over it."

50.

Believe in yourself:
You can find love again.

❧ ❧ ❧

If it is your time love will track you down like a cruise missile.

—LYNDA BARRY

Nobody has only one chance at love. You have as many chances as you are prepared for. You just have to be ready for it.

Your sense of how to love and be loved may have been sent reeling through the shock waves of divorce, but most likely it is intact. You've learned a lot too, about yourself and about what makes a relationship work and not work for you. You haven't messed up your chance at lifelong love—you may have learned how to be better at finding and keeping the real thing.

Love happens for people of all ages. When you have healed enough to take an interest in the outside world and the people in it, they will be interested in you. You really don't have to do anything special, other than to look interested and available. And if you *are* interested and available, that's how you will look.

Timing is an important factor. You won't be able to rush yourself into a workable, makes-sense love affair no matter how much you may want to. You will have to do the work of getting past the hardest parts of the divorce process first, unless by great good fortune you meet someone who has enough patience to endure and wait for you. If you think that finding someone wonderful will help you heal, you may be right, but you may not be able to hold on to that person if you have little but your own needs to offer. Try to be patient.

It's true that as we grow older there are more single women in the world than there are single men. So it's important to remember two things: It only takes one of those men, the right one, of course, to make you part of a pair; and if that man is hard to find, you can still have friendships and interesting companions throughout the rest of your life if you keep yourself open to the possibilities that life sends your way.

Have faith. Think about what you want from love this time, and what you are prepared to give. Being thoughtful and realistic about your needs and your assets will give you a better chance at finding a person, or people, with whom you can share life in the most healthy way, a way that offers the real possibility of fulfillment and joy.

- When you are honestly ready for love, you will give off the right signals without even trying.
- Until real love comes along, you can still enjoy lots of good company.
- Be yourself and you will be loved for the woman you really are.

"I had some very specific ideas about the kind of man I wanted to meet," says Iris, 40. "I wasn't interested in anyone who had never had children, and I much preferred someone who had elementary school age children, as I do. My daughter is seven and I didn't want to try to win over a man who wasn't used to kids, who hadn't thought about them seriously. I haven't done very much to go after guys. I mean, I haven't joined any singles groups or gone anywhere for the purpose of meeting someone. I was very busy with my business and my daughter, keeping the house in order. But I like to socialize and go out and do things, so I was just kind of going about life as usual. One rainy Saturday I took Katie to some caverns that are about an hour south of

here. We were going around with a small group of people, looking at the stalactites and underground pools and all that. I noticed a good-looking man with a couple of little boys trailing along. He looked about the right age, and his kids looked a little younger than Katie. And all through the afternoon, he was never very far away, and I could see him looking at me when I was trying not to let him see me look at him. When we finished our tour, Katie and I stopped for ice cream at the snack bar. And sure enough Craig and his two boys stopped too, and we started to talk. It turned out that he had been separated a little longer than I had, and that we lived only about five miles apart. We've gone on a lot of Saturday outings with our kids over the past year and we have a lot of fun. I'm sorry to say it never became a romance, we're just friends. But not sorry, really because it's great to have a male friend right now. And just recently Craig introduced me to a very sweet and interesting friend of his and we've gone out a couple of times. We'll see! Hey, if I could meet such a good friend as Craig in a cave, who knows what else could come along? We'll see what happens next!"

Resources

୬ ୬ ୬

Few national groups for separated and divorced people exist. You can find support groups in almost any community, but you will have to do a little research. Some logical resources for information about support groups in your area are churches and synagogues, women's centers, family counselors and psychotherapists, and lawyers who specialize in domestic relations.

Even if you don't think of yourself as the support group type, you might want to attend a meeting or two just to get practical information from people who are further along with their separations and divorces. Support group members may provide very useful recommendations of attorneys, counselors, financial advisors, singles clubs, and other sources of assistance for you.

Don't hesitate to ask separated and divorced women for the names of programs or individuals who have been helpful to them. Most women are more than happy to share the benefits of their experience.

Afterword

Every divorce is accompanied by its own unique set of life lessons. The fifty examples here are just a start. You can make something good grow out of the loss of your marriage by paying attention to what you have learned. Talk to other women. Let them know about your experience, offer some of your own advice as the next step to take you further along in your own self-renewal. If you've learned something significant that you would like to pass on, I would be very grateful to hear from you. Please write to me at Avon Books, 1350 Avenue of the Americas, New York, New York 10019.